PARIS

MICHAEL'S GUIDE

PARIS

Series editor:
Michael Shichor

INBAL
Travel Information Ltd.

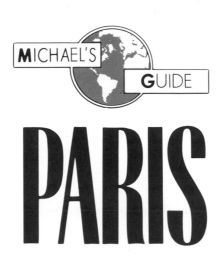

Inbal Travel Information Ltd.
P.O.Box 39090 Tel Aviv Israel 61390

Intl. ISBN 965-288-064-7

Text: Shlomo Papirblat

Distributed in the United Kingdom by:
Kuperard (London) Ltd.
30 Cliff Rd.
London NW1 9AG

U.K. ISBN 1-870668-38-3

CONTENTS

TABLE OF MAPS

MICHAEL'S GUIDE SERIES INCLUDES:

MICHAEL'S GUIDE ARGENTINA, CHILE, PARAGUAY & URUGUAY
MICHAEL'S GUIDE BOLIVIA & PERU
MICHAEL'S GUIDE ECUADOR, COLOMBIA & VENEZUELA
MICHAEL'S GUIDE BRAZIL
MICHAEL'S GUIDE SOUTH AMERICA (Continental)

MICHAEL'S GUIDE NORTHERN CALIFORNIA
MICHAEL'S GUIDE SOUTHERN CALIFORNIA
MICHAEL'S GUIDE CALIFORNIA

MICHAEL'S GUIDE SCANDINAVIA
MICHAEL'S GUIDE SCOTLAND
MICHAEL'S GUIDE SWITZERLAND
MICHAEL'S GUIDE HUNGARY
MICHAEL'S GUIDE TURKEY

MICHAEL'S GUIDE NEW YORK CITY
MICHAEL'S GUIDE LONDON
MICHAEL'S GUIDE PARIS
MICHAEL'S GUIDE AMSTERDAM
MICHAEL'S GUIDE BRUSSELS & ANTWERP
MICHAEL'S GUIDE FRANKFURT
MICHAEL'S GUIDE ROME
MICHAEL'S GUIDE MADRID
MICHAEL'S GUIDE BARCELONA
MICHAEL'S GUIDE JERUSALEM

Preface

Paris is a major destination in the tourist world, and for good reason. It is an enchanting and monumental city, showing the visitor many faces and offering a never ending array of attractions. Paris will captivate the stern-faced art lover, the light-footed nomad, the poet, the homemaker. Paris has everything, from the best in cuisine and entertainment to shopping centers and tourist sites.

Most visitors to Paris keep coming back, time after time, for once you've been caught in its spell the city is hard to overlook. Therefore, we devote an entire book just to Paris, leading the visitor — veteran or newcomer — through all those places which make Paris...Paris.

Much time and thought have gone into selecting and designing informative and interesting tour routes. They present various attractions, restaurants, beautiful cityscapes and anecdotes in a manner suitable for all. This Guide is for the tourist who wishes to know Paris thorough, who aches to absorb sights, tastes, aromas, people. The author, Shlomo Papirblat, is a journalist and sworn "Parisologist". A parisian during his years of study at the Sorbonne, he has since returned again and again.

To produce this Guide, Shlomo crisscrossed Paris for weeks; stalking its museums and libraries, visiting its schools and research institutes, tasting its foods and pleasures, travelling, exploring and sampling the best of Paris. The result is your to enjoy.

After carefully separating the trully essential from the less important, we compiled the mass of material into a concise guide. It takes the tourist through Paris quickly, comfortably and interestingly, making best use of time and resources.

Our efforts will be rewarded if you come away from Paris with a profound affection for the city, a genuine enthusiasm and an appetite for more. In short, we want you to feel exactly as we do.

Michael Shichor

Using this Guide

In order to reap maximum benefit from the information concentrated in this Guide, we advise the traveler to carefully read the following advice and to act upon it. The facts contained in this book are meant to help the tourist fund his or her way around and to assure that he sees the most, with maximum savings of money, time and effort.

The information contained in the Introduction should be read in its entirely as it will supply you with details which will help in making the early decisions and arrangements for your trip. Reviewing the material thoroughly and acting upon it, means that you will be more organized and set for your visit. Upon arrival in Paris, you will already feel familiar and comfortable with it, more so than otherwise would have been the case.

The basic guideline in all "MICHAEL'S GUIDE" publications is to survey places in a primarily geographical sequence. The detailed introductory chapters discuss general topics and specific aspects of getting organized. The tour routes, laid out geographically, lead the visitor up and down the city's streets, providing a survey of the sites and calling attention to all those details which deepen one's familiarity with Paris, and make a visit there so much more enjoyable. At the end of each chapter is a section called "Additional points of interest", which relates to sites located in the vicinity of that tour route.

Following the tour routes is a chapter devoted to the cities and sites on Paris' periphery, taking in the area within several hours travel distance from the city. Relatively few visitors to Paris, it seems, venture out of town. There one finds the "real" France — a creature totally different from Paris, but no less enchanting and pleasurable.

A concise list of "musts" follows, describing those sites without which a visit to Paris is not complete.

The reader will notice that certain facts tend to recur. This is deliberate; it enables the tourist who starts out from a point other than the one we choose, to be no less informed. The result is a flexibility in personal planning.

The rich collection of maps covers the tour routes and special attractions in great detail. Especially prepared for this book, they will certainly add to the efficiency and pleasure of your exploration of Paris.

A concise chapter is provided on shopping, entertainment, restaurants, and the other essences of this city. These will help visitors fill their suitcases and stomachs — and empty their wallets — comprehensively, thoroughly, and as economically as possible. Here again, a broad spectrum of possibilities is provided, taking the budgets of all travelers into consideration (while guaranteeing a healthy dose of enjoyment).

To further facilitate the use of this Guide, we have included a detailed index. It includes all the major sites mentioned throughout the book. Consult the index to find something by name and it will refer you to the place where it is mentioned in greatest detail.

During your visit you will see and experience many things — we have therefore left several blank pages at the back of the Guide. These are for you, to jot down those special experiences of people and places, feelings and significant happenings along the way.

Because times and cities are dynamic, an important rule of thumb when travelling, and when visiting a vibrant city like Paris especially, should be to consult local sources of information. Tourists are liable to encounter certain inaccuracies in this Guide and for these, we apologize.

The producer of a guide of this type assumes a great responsibility; that of presenting the right information in a way which allows for an easy, safe and economical visit. To this end, cooperation and assistance are necessary from those of you who have enjoyed the information contained in this Guide. For this purpose, we have included a short questionnaire and will be most grateful for those who will take the time to complete it and send it to us. A complementary copy of the new edition will be forwarded to those of you whose contribution will appear in the up-dated edition.

Have a pleasant and exciting trip — Bon Voyage!

INTRODUCTION

Part One — A Taste of What's to come

Paris: Under the spell of romance

Paris has an enchanting power — it is very romantic. At the very first sight of its narrow cobbled streets, broad boulevards and open piazzas, it takes the visitor into its embrace. Everyone has a personal Paris, and Paris gives something to everyone.

Paris is an innkeeper with a clientele of centuries, the object of thousands of tumultuous lovers, the receptacle of evil winds of blood and fire. Yet throughout, hers is a youthful profile.

French author Cau described Paris as *a woman with a veil of wisdom over her beautiful face, a face which will look forever like that of a young woman of thirty-five. The Seine drapes about her neck like a brooch of emeralds; her derrière is not too high, not too low; and her bourgeoise makeup cannot hide her promising, hinting naughtiness which beckons you forward. London, Madrid, Moscow, Tokyo, Berlin — these are men. Paris is a woman.*

The Paris of Victor Hugo or Henry Miller, Honoré de Balzac or Ernest Hemingway, Molière or Ionesco, Renoir or Picasso. Paris; the same yet different.

The Paris of political refugees or struggling poets, authors in search of an opening line, or of artists in pursuit of their models. Paris; the same yet different.

Paris of the crisp baguette, of the feathery croissant, of red Bordeaux and clear champagne. Paris of restaurants — Russian, Chinese, North African, Jewish... So French, so cosmopolitan.

The elegance of the Champs-Elysées, the vulgarity of Pigalle, the intriguing Latin Quarter, the bourgeoise Paris of Boulevard Foch. The Paris of the Louvre, of Galeries Lafayette. Paris; the same yet different. The Paris of the Great Debate: a city which was, now in decline, or is its future still to come? Hated by some, loved, revered and admired by many, Paris continues to cast its unique and eternal spell.

A capsule history

Place Dauphine, on Ile de la Cité, embraced on all sides by the Seine is where Paris began. Sometime during the 3rd century BC, members of a Celtic tribe, the **Parisii**, set up a little village on the island and called it Lokostia (Water Colony). However, the Parisii's humble cabins had to go if the place was to become a real city. The task was handled by the conquering army of Julius Caesar in 52 BC. The Romans installed the fixed standards of their civilization — temples, a forum, an amphitheater, large houses with baths, an aqueduct — on the left bank of the Seine. The city was called **Lutétia**. Only a few relics, none too impressive, survive from this era. They include ruins of the amphitheater on Rue Monge, a bath near Musée Cluny, and traces of the aqueduct in Arcueil, outside today's city limits. One remnant of Lutétia, however, not only survived but is prominent on almost every street corner today: the boat symbol of the city of Paris, recalling the important commercial river port which Lutétia had once been.

In the 3rd century AD St. Denis reached Paris. Although he was executed shortly thereafter, he gave the area its first taste of Christianity. Toward mid-century, the city expanded greatly. It became a strategic center and two Roman Emperors, Julian and his successor, Valentinian I — were actually crowned there. By that time the city had become known as **Parisia**.

The Huns conquered Parisia in the 5th century. They were succeeded by the Merovingians, who made it their capital, and then by the Carolingians.

At the end of the 10th century, Parisia was chosen by Hugh Capet, founder of the royal Capetian line, as his seat of operations. As Capet's strength grew, his city gradually became the most important one in France.

Paris took a leap forward in the 11th century. **The Ville**, a commercial and artisan quarter, came into being on the right bank of the Seine and the **Church of St.-Germain-des-Prés** was built on the foundations of a 6th-century abbey. Construction of the **Cathedral of Notre-Dame** commenced. During the 12th century, Philip II built a siege wall around Paris (pop. approx. 100,000 at the time) and erected the fortress known as **the Louvre** at the city's western extremity.

After a brief English occupation during the Hundred Years War, Paris returned to its grandeur. Its population doubled (to approx. 200,000) during the reign of Francois I, making Paris the largest city in Europe.

A building boom under Henry IV (late 16th century) gave Paris its first stone bridge over the Seine — **Le Pont Neuf** (the New Bridge) which is the oldest bridge spanning the Seine today. In 1635, Cardinal Richelieu established **L'Académie Française** in Paris, thus laying the foundation on which Paris developed into a great cultural center. By the end of that century it included the Academy for the Sciences and the Academy for Literature.

In 1682, Louis XIV established his residence in Versailles, near Paris. Fearful for his personal security, he chose to leave the city which he considered too rebellious. It was during his reign though, that Paris' development reached a new pinnacle. A population of 400,000 thronged its streets. Its walls were leveled and replaced with broad thoroughfares. A municipal police force was established, a public transportation system began to evolve and street lights became commonplace. Such innovations were unheard of elsewhere in Europe.

By 1774 however, when Louis XVI ascended the throne, France had deteriorated alarmingly. The populace, under conventional practice at the time, was divided into three "estates" or classes — the First Estate (the clergy), the Second Estate (the nobility), and the Third Estate (the proletariate). Expressed in numbers, the First and Second Estates accounted for about one million people, leaving some 24 million in the Third Estate.

Wasteful spending had exhausted the state exchequer. Most of France's wealth had gone either for war or for heavy payments to thousands of noblemen at the royal court. The King preferred to keep them nearby, in artificially created positions to prevent interference in matters of government.

In order to increase the flow of funds to the royal accounts, more taxes were imposed on the Third Estate. Considering that the earnings of the laborers and peasants were negligible to begin with, the new levies often brought them to the point of starvation. It is estimated that more than one million Frenchmen subsisted as beggars at the time.

Count D'Angero, in a letter written in 1750, describes the Paris he found in a tone of refined disgust: *"Thousands of people creep about in the streets in search of some bread, lest they starve to death. Things have reached such a state that some survive on grass."*

The situation being such, the masses decided there was no alternative but to make their own justice, which resulted in the French Revolution. This was the first insurrection of its scale and the bloodiest known in the annals of history to that time.

On June 23, 1789, representatives of the Third Estate assembled and demanded that the King give France a new constitution guaranteeing freedom and equality of political rights to all citizens, irrespective of class or origin. Louis XVI's first thought was to order them to disperse. Fearing a mass rampage in Paris and Versailles, however, he decided on a tactical maneuver. On June 27, he invited representatives of the clergy and the nobility to join the Third Estate delegates in a National Assembly which would rewrite the laws of France.

But the social snowball had already built up too much momentum. Throughout France peasants and workers stormed the palaces of noblemen, assaulting their occupants and destroying property. A frightened Louis XVI brought troops to Versailles and Paris, fearing that the riots would reach these locations as well. The National Assembly insisted that the soldiers be removed from the cities and by refusing, the royal court struck match to gunpowder.

The symbolic peak of the revolution was on July 14, 1789. Much of the population of the French capital, 600,000 strong, seized pitchforks, shovels and weapons acquired during their looting, and stormed the **Bastille** — a fortress-prison for political offenders. After a bloody battle, the Parisians penetrated the fortress, massacred the royal guardsmen and freed the prisoners. In the wake of the Paris example, riots and insurrections broke out throughout France.

At this stage, Louis XVI was still trying to save his throne. He announced that he was siding with the people in their struggle for equal rights and ratified the Declaration of Human and Civil Rights which the National Assembly had adopted on August 26, 1789. Behind the scenes however, he plotted and schemed with the rulers of Austria and Prussia, arranging for expeditionary forces which would save his throne.

In order to join his allies as they prepared their invasion, Louis XVI attempted to flee France on the night of June 20, 1791 On the way, near the town of **Varenne**, he was identified, arrested and sent back to Paris.

In June 1792, as the enemy armies advanced into French territory, the rebels accused the King of treason. In August of that year, they burst into the palace at Versailles and declared an end to the monarchy. The general enthusiasm of the populace fueled the morale of the revolutionary army and this competently commanded force went out to repel the invading European armies. On September 20, in a decisive battle, the Prussian army was forced to retreat. On November 6, as news reached Paris that the revolutionary army had crossed into Belgium, the Revolutionary Government announced the birth of the French Republic.

Louis XVI was sentenced to death a month later "for conspiring against the freedom of the nation." On January 21, 1793, he was sent to the guillotine at **Place de la Révolution** (today's **Place de la Concorde**).

The reaction to the King's execution by the other monarchs of Europe was one of outrage. Fearing the French example, the rulers of England, Russia, Spain, Portugal and Holland joined forces with Austria and Prussia against France.

These developments provoked some of the French, whose fervor had begun to diminish. They voiced grave allegations against the revolutionaries for ordering the execution of the King and for causing the enmity of all of Europe. When the issue actually sparked riots in several cities, the radical revolutionary faction responded with force. Led by a lawyer named Maximilio Robespierre, a Committee of Public Safety came into being. It was Robespierre's job to execute those suspected of disloyalty to the revolution. Between July 1793 and July 1794, a period known as the

Reign of Terror in French history, thousands were sent to the guillotine. Revolutionaries who opposed his methods arrested Robespierre on July 27, 1794, and sent him to the guillotine the next day.

It took until 1795 to create the French constitution based on human and civil rights which was adopted by the National Assembly in 1789. The new codex represented a triumph of principles which were to influence many nations in subsequent eras.

Though the Revolution effectively spent itself by the end of that year, France and the monarchies of Europe, led by Austria, were still at war. This situation suited the new Government of France. They saw the possibility of achieving domination over the wealthy cities of Italy which would reinvigorate the sickly French exchequer.

Command of the army stationed on the Italian border was entrusted to a young general named Napoleon Bonaparte. The Corsican-born officer used the military academy in Paris (he had graduated in 1785 as number 42 in a class of 51), as a springboard to the throne of Emperor, which he established in Paris in 1804.

It was Napoleon who catalyzed Paris' recovery after years of war. Upon return, he gathered the reins of power, and initiated the construction of opulent memorials (such as the **Arc de Triomphe de l'Etoile** and the **Church of the Madeleine**).

The man who made a truly great impact on Paris, however, was Baron Georges Eugene Haussmann, and it was he who orchestrated the revitalization of Paris and his mark is evident to this day. Haussmann, a jurist by training and son of a Protestant family from Alsace, was a political supporter of Napoleon III while serving in 1851 as Prefect of the Bordeaux District. After Napoleon III became Emperor, Haussmann was reassigned to the Seine, an important district which included the capital, Paris.

During his 17 years in this position, Haussmann built the "new Paris." In deciding to level the ancient slums, he had several considerations in mind. One was an answer to mass unemployment problems; another was the eradication of the labyrinthine alleyways which had sheltered groups of rebels. Haussmann replaced the houses with broad, straight, paved boulevards, punctuated with spacious plazas and embellished with gardens and trees.

He improved transportation in Paris immeasurably, sponsored the city's belt railway, and improved the sewer system and water supply. City limits were expanded by annexing adjacent neighborhoods and suburbs. Public and government buildings were erected and ironically, he established the Service for the Preservation of Paris Antiquities.

During the dynamic Baron's tenure, the population of Paris ballooned to about two million. The primacy of Paris in France's economy, business and culture strengthened. Nevertheless, the hundreds of millions of francs in public funds spent on all this activity aggravated the general tax burden and subjected Haussmann to fierce criticism from the political left. Haussmann was dismissed as Prefect when his patron, Napoleon III, suffered a defeat to Prussia in 1870 and lost his throne to the Third Republic. Paris was once again faced with a difficult period of war and bloodshed.

In 1871, the Franco-Prussian War subjected Paris to a cruel, four-month siege until the city fell to Germany. Harsher yet, were the atrocities of the Paris Commune — an agglomeration of anti-reconciliation patriots who wanted to pursue Germany even after peace had been negotiated and the capital restored to French control. When the French Republican Government sent troops against them, 20,000 were killed, and the City Hall and **Palais des Tuileries** were torched.

However, Paris quickly recovered and resumed its growth. The city opera house was completed in 1874. Paris hosted large international expositions in 1879, 1889 and 1900 which attracted multitudes of tourists from throughout Europe.

During World War I, Paris was bombarded by artillery and from the air, but the city was not taken. At the end of the war, peace treaties between the Allies and the Central Powers were signed in nearby **Versailles**. During World War II, Paris came under Nazi occupation early in 1940. The city was liberated four years later by American forces reinforced by General de Gaulle's Free French.

After World War II, the Fourth Republic was declared and, despite many political difficulties, held together until 1958. Then, collapsing in a crisis precipitated by the war in Algeria, the parliamentary regime gave way to the Fifth Republic, a strongly presidential system inaugurated by de Gaulle. During this period, the central role played by Paris was strengthening. It took a decisive part in the economic, commercial and cultural life of France, as well as in the political system and government. This resulted in an large influx of French into the surrounding area. The people remained in the suburbs around Paris, rather than in the city itself. This resulted in a broadening belt of peripheral towns, or outer suburbs, many of which were built in haste, without much care, resulting in gray "slumber-cities."

In May 1968, Paris was swept by turbulent demonstrations and street battles — students and workers on one side, security forces on the other. De Gaulle was routed in the following year's elections; his successor, Georges Pompidou, galvanized vast public works to improve the city's profile.

Paris' twenty *arrondissements* (*quartiers*) were unified in 1977; since which time Jacques Chirac has been elected and re-elected Mayor. According to the system of municipal elections, each *quartier* elects its own "mayor." They, in turn, along with the muncipal councils, choose the mayor of Paris.

Valéry Giscard d'Estaing, who became president after the death of Georges Pompidou, and current President François Mitterand, have continued in the tradition of supporting and promoting innovations throughout Paris.

Paris topography

Paris is situated in northwestern France on the River Seine, 230 miles (373 km) from the mouth of the Seine at the English Channel. Its area is approximately 40 sq. miles (104 sq. km). Most of the city is flat, the highest point is Montmartre (elev. 128 m). The Seine splits in two in the center of town, sandwiching two islands — **Ile de la Cité** and **Ile St. Louis.**

Downtown Paris, the city's oldest section, covers a mere 5 sq. miles (14 sq. km) and is relatively easy to explore. It is ringed by the city's major railroad stations: **St. Lazare, Nord**, **Est**, **Lyon**, **Austerlitz** and **Montparnasse**. Downtown encompasses 10 *quartiers* of the city and houses the institutions of government, public affairs, education and culture, and most of the city's commerce.

Past downtown, the area to the north and northeast is populated by workers and immigrants of low economic standing. The southern *quartiers* are devoted primarily to light industry and commerce. Galleries and popular leisure and entertainment spots are found in Montmartre, in *Quartier* 18. In the northwest, are *Quartiers* 16 and 17, prestige residential areas featuring mansions originally built for the nobility.

Though Paris is a densely built up city, its broad avenues, boulevards and spacious plazas allow it some breathing space. The important parks are **Tuileries**, **Luxembourg**, **Jardin des Plantes**, **Champ-de-Mars**, **Montsouris** and **Monceau.**

It is worthwhile and interesting to know that today's Parisians inherited much of Baron Haussman's attitude. They yearn for constant activity, change, tremendous projects, innovation. Upon returning to Paris after an absence of several years, one can find certain streets, if not entire areas, transformed beyond recognition. A good example in recent years is the **Les Halles** area where the produce market of Paris was established in the 12th century. Emile Zola labelled the massive, picturesque enterprise "the belly of Paris". Cinema lovers may remember it as the major setting for *Irma la Douce*, produced in the 1960s. Between 1960 and 1979, the marketplace was pushed outside the city limits and replaced with a monumental, prestige shopping center. Its four subterranean floors, encased in glass and aluminium, house 200 shops, 10 cinemas, 12 restaurants and a museum.

The traits behind the phenomenon — momentum, skill and ability — ensure that Paris will not stagnate in coming years. Many places around town will assume new characters and profiles, and signs of such changes are already evident.

Plans for the 1990s are directed towards addressing one of the biggest problems facing the French capital. About 10 million people live in Paris' outer suburbs (constituting a fifth of the population of France). The majority of Parisians work in the city and this has resulted in extreme traffic and transportation problems for the millions of workers streaming into the city each day.

A number of plans have been formulated to ease the traffic congestion. Another highway is to be constructed in addition to the existing one. The new highway will form an even larger ring around the city, to include the nearer outlying areas, in the hope of reducing the vehicular traffic flowing through the city gates. Another approach is to encourage large companies, which employ tens of thousands of workers, to move their offices outside Paris.

To somewhat alleviate the extreme parking problems, huge underground parking garages are under construction, including one beneath the Jardin des Tuileries. Another suggested possibility is, once again, to use the Seine as a channel for in-town transportion. The idea here is that barges will transport passengers to stations along the river banks. This would, of course, suit people who live and work within walking distance of the Seine. This is not a novel idea, in the 1920s the river was used for public transportation, but has since been neglected and forgotten.

Climate

Paris usually has an agreeable climate. The city sits on the dividing line between northern and southern Europe and combines the climatic characteristics of each. It is hard to speak of clearly defined seasons. Autumn can be rainy, very rainy or partly cloudy. Though winter brings a few snowy days, the snow usually melts at once. Temperatures fluctuate around 10°C (50°F). Spring is a rainy period interspersed with beautiful days. Summer can be oppressively hot and is punctuated by occasional thunderstorms and downpours. Fortunately, Paris enjoys frequent westerly winds which prevent the serious build up of air pollution which plagues other large cities. In terms of weather, when should you visit Paris? There is no answer; it depends on luck.

Architecture

Every epoch in the history of architecture has left its imprint on Paris. Even so, the city's various sites co-exist in harmony, instead of the eclectic jumble one might expect. The different styles complement one another and create a rich, interesting mosaic.

Of the few ruins which have survived from the early Roman period (see "A Capsule History"), the most noteworthy is the Cluny Bathhouse, at the intersection of St. Michel and

St. Germain Blvds. In contrast, quite a few of the many monasteries and churches dating from the early Middle Ages have been preserved.

Construction of the **Cathedral of Notre-Dame** began in 1163 and continued until 1250, and the result reflects a transition to Gothic style. Notre-Dame served as an example for all of Europe, and was often imitated. An additional and exceptional example of early Gothic style is the **Basilica of St. Denis**, just north of Paris.

These and other churches express the achievements attained by the Gothic style in architecture, painting and sculpture. The stained glass windows, of course, should also be noted. The period's artists turned these into "books" of sorts, illustrated with scenes from the Old and New Testaments. A wonderful example of stained glass art is in the **Church of La Sainte Chapelle**, built in the 13th century by Louis IX (St. Louis).

The Renaissance style was introduced to Paris by François I. With the help of his architect, François I built the court of **Hôtel La Cour Carrée** and the inner court of **Hôtel Carnavalet**. The latter houses a museum of Paris history from its earliest days to the Renaissance.

Baroque style, a product of early 17th-century Italy, never caught on in Paris. Of the very few Paris sites reminiscent of this style, two may be mentioned: **l'Eglise St. Paul** and **Le Collège des Quatre Nations**, the present home of l'Académie Française.

The neo-classical style of the late 18th Century swept Europe in a reaction against Baroque and a desire to return to the ways of old. Examples are the **Church of the Madelaine** with its Greek temple lines, and **Arc de Triomphe** in Place de l'Etoile. The French call this "First Empire" style, referring, of course, to Napoleon.

An impressive example of Second Empire style, dating from the late 19th century, is the **Paris Opera House**. Its architect, Garnier, defined it as "Napoleon III style" and Napoleon himself did not overlook the compliment.

Art Nouveau reached Paris in the early 20th century and with it the propensity for engraving various floral themes and intertwining branches in metal and stone. The first metro (subway) was built at this time, and certain station entrances with Art Nouveau embellishments may still be seen today.

The functional Modern style of the inter-war period, which succeeded in preserving the spirit of grandeur in architecture, is also amply evident in Paris. One example is **Palais de Chaillot.** Built for an international exposition in 1937, it reflects the great enthusiasm with which the architects of the time adopted the new building materials of concrete and steel.

The most conspicuous structures of recent years are the skyscrapers of glass, lightweight metal and precast concrete in **Montparnasse**, **Quartier La Défense**, the **Pompidou Center**, the new **Les Halles** shopping center and the **Science Complex** at La Défense.

Paris in Numbers

Dimensions (as the crow flies): 7.5 miles (12 km) x 5.5 miles (9 km)
Longest street: rue Vaugirard, 2.5 miles (4.2 km)
Shortest street: rue Degres, 20 ft. (6 m)
Widest street: Bd Foch, 400 ft (120 m)
Narrowest street: Chat qui Pêche, 8 ft. (2.5 m)
Oldest house: 3 rue Volta, constructed in 1407
Oldest tree: Vivani St., planted in about 1600
Tallest structure: the Eiffel Tower, 1050 ft. (320 m)
Tallest building: Montparnasse Tower, 400 ft. (120m)
Population: 2,177,000 (46% men, 54% women) according to latest census (1982)
Most populous *quartier*: the *Quartier* 15, with 225,000 residents
Least populous *quartier:* the *Quartier* 1, with 19,000 residents
Foreign residents: 370,000
Average temperature (last 30 years): 11.5°C
Average number of snowy days: 15
Average number of days at or over 30°C: 6
Number of shops: 67,000
Number of museums: 85
Number of cinemas: 500 (122,000 seats)
Number of theaters; 61
Number of concert halls: 48

Part Two — Setting out

When to come

Visit Paris whenever you can. Objectively speaking, the Paris **Office de Tourisme** has found that certain times of the year are more "touristy" than others. The following periods are considered peak tourist seasons: February 1-4, 15-19; March 9-16; April 14-27; May 8-18, 27-31; June 1-4; July-October. If you are planning to arrive during these periods, you should book all flight and hotel reservations well in advance.

There are other factors to be taken into account, depending on personal preferences. During the summer months of July and August, Paris is, to a certain extent, unlike Paris the rest of the year. This is the period of the *vacances*, when many Parisians leave for their annual vacations. According to statistics, 500,000 Parisians leave the city in July, and 700,000 during the month of August! Although this makes it easier to find parking in the city, many places are closed during these months. One must also remember that 2.5 million tourists visit Paris during July and August.

Holy days and holidays

Paris celebrates the following holidays each year:

January 1: New Year's Day.
End of March (varies); second day of Easter.
May 1: Labor Day.
May 8: Fête de la Libération.
May 8 (varies): l'Ascension, commemorating the ascension of Jesus to heaven.
May 19 (varies): Le Lundi de Pentecôte (Pentecost).
July 14: Bastille Day, a national holiday.
August 15: l'Assomption, "Virgin's Day".
November 1: La Toussaint, All Saints'Day.
November 11: Armistice Day (end of World War I).
December 25: Noël (Christmas).

Expect most museums, offices and department stores to be closed on these days. Public transportation schedules are scaled down. For many restaurants, cafes and shops it is business as usual.

Documents

France requires that most foreigners have entry visas. The visas must be obtained at a French Consulate prior to departure, as they are not given at the border.

Visas are generally given for periods of six months and in order to extend it (for which you need a good reason), contact the Service for Alien Affairs in Paris at the Ministry of Police, 163 rue de Charenton, 12^{e}, tel. 43.41.81.49.

Drivers must have an international driver's license. It is recommended to keep it together with your own license.

An International Student Card is good for discounts and first claim to space in youth hostels. At times, without any particular regularity, it allows discounts on admission to museums and cinemas. Present it everywhere; it often proves useful in unexpected places.

Insurance

Even if Paris is one of the world's centers of culture, visitors should carry health and luggage insurance. Gangs of muggers have admittedly vanished since the French Revolution, but theft occurs here as anywhere and the uninsured victim is likely to come away with a total loss. Health coverage is even more important. Medical care and hospitalization are expensive when paid out of pocket, especially if an emergency flight home is involved. So don't leave such vital matters to luck.

Customs

French law permits anyone entering the country for less than six months to import personal effects with no limitation. However, tourists are supposed to carry purchase receipts for valuables such as cameras, video gear, watches, etc. (the requirement is rarely enforced.)

Duty-free goods are permitted in limited quantities. For example, one may bring 200 cigarettes, 150 cigarillos, 50 cigars or 250 grams of tobacco. For alcohol, the limits are one liter of liquor over 22 proof, or two liters under 22 proof, plus two liters of wine. As for perfume, only 50 ml is permitted.

The import of drugs, weapons and gold is totally prohibited by law.

How much will it cost?

This is the hardest question of all to answer. Of the 13-14 million tourists who come here each year, most spend some 500-2,000 francs per day each (including meals, museums, entertainment and lodging).

The Japanese head the list for the biggest spenders, averaging 2,000f a day. They are followed by the Americans, the Swiss and the Canadians, who spend about 1000f each daily. The English make do with 917f, while the Dutch and Spanish get by on only 780f. Most thrifty are the Germans who spend a mere 640f per day.

Beyond statistics, it all depends on your selection of hotel (if any), entertainment, restaurants, etc. Study the many examples provided below (all prices approximate) and reach a rough estimate.

Expensive

Four/five-star hotel with breakfast — 1200f.
Two meals in good restaurants, fixed-price menu — 600f.
Travel by taxi (three average in-town trips) — 120f.
Visits to two museums or other sites where admission is charged — 45f.
Nightclub (Moulin Rouge, for example), without dinner — 365f.
TOTAL: 2330f ("expensive", can be immeasurably steeper than this).

Moderate

Three-star hotel with breakfast — 400f.
Two full average meals, fixed-price menu, average restaurants — 300f.
Carfare (weekly *Carte-Orange*, i.e., unlimited-trip ticket for metro and bus) — 7f per day.
Visits to two museums or other sites where admission is charged — 45f.
Movie — 35f
TOTAL: 787f.

Inexpensive

One-star hotel with breakfast (sleeping in gardens and parks is forbidden) — 120f.
One hot meal in a fixed-price menu restaurant — 70f.
Another meal in a fast-food establishment or cafe — 30f.
Travel — 7f per day.
Visits to two museums or other sites where admission is charged — 45f.
Movie — 35f.
TOTAL: 307f.

Part Three — Where have we landed?

Transportation

Airports

From **Roissy-Charles-de-Gaulle Airport**, situated about 15 miles (25 km) north of the city, a train leaves every 15 minutes, 5:30am-11:30pm, for Gare du Nord (Paris North Station). Fare: 26f.

A special airport bus, which leaves every few minutes, connects the different terminals with the departure point of the train, a very convenient service.

Air France buses leave every 12 minutes, 5:45am-11pm, picking up passengers from the different terminals, bound for Porte Maillot, Palais des Congrès and then Etoile Square in Paris. Buses depart from Gates 34, 36, A5,B6. Travel time is approximately 40 minutes. Fare: 36 f.

Buses 350 and 351 reach Gare du Nord and Place de la Nation in Paris. Though slower, they are the least expensive mode of transport. Fare 4.40f per ticket (tickets are bought in packs of six).

A taxi (find them in regular and organized stations, without wildcats) is the most convenient way of reaching any address in Paris and the vicinity. It is also the most costly. Fare: 160f (at least) during regular-fare hours.

Hitchhiking is not recommended. French drivers, naturally perhaps, do not like to stop for someone who's laden with packs or suitcases (if they stop for anyone). You may waste a lot of time waiting. If your heart is set on it anyway, make up a little sign indicating your destination.

From **Orly Airport**, located some 10 miles (16 km) south of the city, the RER suburb train runs every 10-15 minutes from Aéroport d'Orly Station to several stations in Paris, including Gare d'Austerlitz. Fare: 19f.

Air France buses set out every 12 minutes, 5:45am-11pm, on a half-hour trip to the Montparnasse train station and then to the terminal at Aérogare des Invalides. Departure from Orly Sud (South) opposite Gate J and Orly Ouest (West) opposite Gate E. Fare: 29f.

Buses 215, 285 and 183. This is the slowest way to go. Stops in Paris include Denfert-Rochereau. Fare: 17.50f for 6 tickets.

Taxi service, again, is orderly, well organized and expensive. Fares begin at 100f during regular-fare hours. As for hitchhiking, see above.

All the above is true in reverse, for the trip back to the airport.

Railway stations

Paris may also be reached by rail via the French National Railways: **Société Nationale des Chemins de Fer Français (SNCF)**. The SNCF offers a wide range of routes throughout France and is linked with other national rails systems. The train network is centered around Paris and the city can easily be reached by rail whether coming from within France or from other cities and towns in Europe. Information regarding SNCF routes and fares, tel. 48.82.50.50 (general information) and tel. 42.80.04.04 (international information).

The major SNCF stations in Paris and trains to and from the city are listed below.

Gare de l'Est: Trains from eastern France. Rail lines from Austria, Germany, Luxembourg and Switzerland.
Gare de Lyon: Trains from the Riviera and southeast France. Rail lines from Greece, Italy and Switzerland.
Gare d'Austerlitz: Trains from central France and the southern Atlantic coast. Rail lines from Portugal and Spain.
Gare Montparnasse: Trains from western France (Chartres, Loire, Valley and Brittany.
Gare du Nord: Trains from the northern coast of France. Rail lines from Belgium, Britain, Germany, Holland and the Scandinavian countries.

All stations are part of the Paris metro system and have bus lines to the city.

In-town transportation

Paris is a very compact city with a total length of about

7.5 miles (12 km) as the crow flies. Its public transportation system is undoubtedly one of the world's finest and efficient use of it saves a great deal of time and money.

Le Métro
With its 15 lines, 360 stations and more than 4 million travelers per day, it is easy to use. Directions are clearly marked and displayed: lines are called by their first and last stations (or vice-versa), and each line is numbered. To reach a certain stop and find the correct metro line, draw an imaginary line on the metro map to the end. The name of the last station is the desired direction. If the destination is not served by any direct line, find the intersection of the line you are on and that which reaches your destination. Switch trains at that intersection. Directions are clearly marked on the platforms and in the corridors as well. Although it may seem complicated at first glance, everything will become clearer and simple after a day or two.

Every metro train has five cars: a first-class car in the middle and two second-class cars on either end. Second-class ticket holders who get caught in first-class between 9am-5pm are fined (though at other times it is permissible). Keep your ticket until you leave the station.

The metro runs from 5:30am-12:30am (this is when the last train starts its final trip). Schedules slow down in the evenings and on Sundays to every 10-15 minutes, as opposed to every 5 minutes or so the rest of the time.

Individual tickets cost 4.40f, and are not really worthwhile. A better deal is the ten-ride ticket (*un carnet)*, which can be purchased for 29.60f. One ticket permits travel on all metro lines, including all necessary transfers.

For a period of a week or a month, the *Carte Orange* is best. This ticket is purchased at any metro station. The procedure, which requires a passport photo, takes only 2-3 minutes. The *Carte Orange*, an extremely useful and economical device, permits unlimited travel on all lines in Paris. Prices: 48f per week, from Monday to Monday, and 167f per month, from the beginning to the end of the month. Ask for a 2-zone card for Paris. This is a permanent card which is kept in a special plastic sleeve together with the individual tickets one buys on each occasion.

Bus
With 56 lines, about 1,700 stops, and more than 4,000 vehicles with comfortable, upholstered chairs, this service is a wonderful way to explore Paris. The drawback is that it is slow, and one risks getting caught in traffic.

Every bus stop has a sign explaining the line and all its stops in full detail. Part of the route is in one color, part in another. Travel "within" one of the colors requires one ticket; a longer trip requires an additional ticket. A *Carte Orange* permits unlimited travel on all Paris lines. Most buses run every day until 8:30pm. There are fewer buses on Sunday. Certain buses run as late as 12.30am and the *Noctambus* lines run all through the night.

RER: This is the rapid and comfortable suburban railroad which crisscrosses the Paris area and reaches destinations near the city proper. Its use requires the purchase of one ticket or more, in addition to the *Carte Orange* (2 zones). Of course, if you are staying outside of Paris, you will need to purchase the applicable *Carte Orange* for 3, 4 or 5 zones, depending on the distance.

Taxi
14,300 cabs, 700 stations, more than 1 million fares per week. Regulations allow a cab to stop only within 55 yards (50 m) of a station. In practice however, Parisians wave them down everywhere. A minimum fare of 8f appears as the meter begins to run. Between 9pm-6:30am and on Sunday, the driver multiplies the meter fare by a special formula. There is also an extra charge for every suitcase and for trips beginning at train stations. The standard tip, *pourboire*, or "drinking money", is 10% of the meter fare. Note! Taxi drivers take only up to three passengers, only occasionally agreeing to a fourth.

Everyone has heard stories of how taxi drivers can turn a 10-minute trip into a half-hour trek. True or not, it's worth looking at a city map, studying the distance involved and gauging the logical time and distance of the trip. The guidelines for working out the tariff are as follows: a trip within the city between 7am-8pm, Tariff A, is 2.55f per km. After 8pm, Tariff B is 3.97f per km. On Sunday it is Tariff B all day. The trip to (or from) either of the airports, Charles de Gaulle or Orly, is calculated according to the regular tariff within the city. On leaving the city it goes up to Tariff B during the day, or Tariff C, 5.33 per km, at night. The driver will add an additional 3-4f in the following situations: if the trip begins from a taxi rank at one of the train stations, for each suitcase or large parcel, for a fourth passenger, for a cat or a dog. For information about parcels left inside a taxi, call tel. 45.31.14.80, ext. 4208.

It is highly advisable not to take cabs during rush hour (7:30-9:30am and 5-7pm), when the possibility of spending endless minutes stuck in traffic, with the meter running, becomes a probability. To order a cab by phone (be prepared to wait up to fifteen minutes), tel. 42.00.67.89, 47.30.23.23., 42.03.99.99., 47.39.33.33., 42.70.41.41., 42.05.77.77. or 42.70.44.22. In addition to the regular price of the trip, the cost of the journey from the point where the taxi was ordered is added on.

Car rentals
Driving within the city is not easy and parking is often very difficult to find. Be aware that the speed limit is 60 kph within town, 80 kph on the ring road around Paris and 130 kph on the highways. Seatbelts are mandatory, and children are required to sit in the back seat. You must always give right of way to vehicles from the right, unless there is a sign to the contrary. To obtain nationwide information on road conditions, call tel. 48.58.33.33. The maximum alcohol level permitted to drivers is 0.8 grams.

Rent-a-car agencies require an international driver's license, and rarely rent to anyone under the age of 21.

Major rent-a-car companies with offices in Paris and at the airports are:

Avis: 5 rue Bixio, 7e, tel. 45.50.32.31.
Hertz: 92 rue St-Lazare, 9e, tel. 42.80.35.45.
Europcar: 48 rue de Berri, 8e, tel. 45.63.04.27.
Budget: 4 av. F. Roosevelt, 8e, tel. 42.25.79.89.
Thrifty: 20, rue de la Folie Méricourt, 11e, tel.43.55.13.00.

Bicycle rental
Below are several companies which rent bicycles.

Vélo-Paris: 2 rue du Fer à Moulin, 5e, tel. 43.37.59.22. Minimum rental one day.

Motorcycle and scooter rental: A license is required to rent a motorcycle but not to rent a scooter.

Market Moto: 19 Place du Marché-Saint-Honoré, 1er, tel. 42.61.09.62. One can also rent a scooter for a weekend, a week or a month from 8 bd. St-Germain, 5e, tel. 46.34.28.10 or 11, rue St-Augustin, 2e, tel. 42.61.72.92.

Helicopter tours: Information on helicopter rentals and tours may be obtained from the firm listed below:

Paris-Helicoptère: Heliport de Paris, 15e, tel. 45.54.12.55.

Transportation and culture

Certain metro stations in Paris stage exhibitions on different themes, and exhibit reproductions of artistic works on the platforms. You can get off at these stations to look at the art, and then continue your journey on the next train. The stations are: Louvre, Hôtel de Ville, St-Germain des Près and Varenne. As always with the metro, changes and additions are expected.

Deciphering Paris Addresses

This guide contains numerous useful addresses. Just the same, mere numbers are not enough. Below is an explanation and a brief glossary of the various terms used.

9, rue Fragonard, 17e

The house number comes first. A great many houses along Paris streets abut one another, adding up to one long building. Every entrance has its own number, followed by the street designation — Rue, Blvd., etc. House numbers start nearest to the Seine, increasing as you move away from the river. For streets that run parallel to the river, the house numbers increase in the direction that the river flows (east-west). Even numbers are on the right, and odd numbers on the left, when looking up to the street in the direction of the numbering. Be aware that a street (rue) and a boulevard may share the same name — such as rue Montmartre and Bd. Montmartre.

The name itself comes next, followed by the number of the municipal *quartier* — 17e in the case above. This information sometimes appears in a different form: 75017, for example. In this case, 750 is the postal code for all of Paris; and 17 is the *quartier* number.

When a metro station appears in an address, it is always the closest station to the address, not necessarily the easiest to reach. Consult a metro map to see if there is a shorter or more convenient way to get there from where you are.

Glossary

(including standard abbreviations)

Avenue — *Avenue* (Av.)
Boulevard — *Boulevard* (Bd.)
Junction/intersection — *Carrefour* (Carr.)
Town/complex — *Cité*
Covered street — *Galerie*
Dead-end street — *Impasse* (Imp.)
Alley, passageway — *Passage*
Square, plaza — *Place* (Pl.)
Bridge — *Pont*
City entrance, gate — *Porte* (Pte.)
Platform, dock, river bank — *Quai*
Street — *Rue* (R.)
Alley/lane/path — *Ruelle*
Square — *Rond-Point* (Rd.-Pt.)
Courtyard, public garden — *Square* (Sq.)
Church — *Eglise*
Garden — *Jardin*
Park — *Parc*
Forest, wood — *Bois, Forêt*
Suburb — *Faubourg*
Courtyard — *Cour*
Estate, private home — *Villa*
Lane (garden) — *Allée*
Road — *Route*

Accommodation

Paris has lodging possibilities to meet every visitor's needs and budget. There are about 3,800 hostelries, including more than 1,300 which are recognized and ranked by the French *Office de Tourisme* with a total of some 135,000 rooms. Prices are fixed by classification, location and services offered.

One must still plan with the knowledge that, on average, the cost of hotels in Paris is the highest in Europe. There is not much one can do about this, but two points are worth bearing in mind. It is always cheaper to visit during the off-season. During the peak season, from May 1st to October 31st, hotel tariffs are about 30% higher. Also, check a few hotels within the star-rating you're looking for. There are no restrictions on hotel tariffs, so make enquiries before selecting a particular hotel. Examples of prices follow, ranked by "star" and location:

4-star deluxe hotel in Quartier 1: Single: up to 2,000f, breakfast 95f extra; double: up to 2,450f.
4-star hotel in Quartier 8: Single: 1,000f, breakfast 70f extra; double: 1,5000f.
3-star hotel in Quartier 6: Single: 500f, breakfast 40f extra; double: 1,000f.
2-star hotel in Quartier 5: Single: 350f, breakfast 20f extra; double: 450f.
1-star hotel in Quartier 9: Single: 250f, breakfast 20f extra; double: 350f.

Before selecting a hotel, be aware of several peculiarly French problems involved. In 1 to 3-star hotels, the level of expectations does not always stand in direct proportion to ranking. That is, two hotels of equivalent rank may be distinctly different in terms of service, facilities and quality of rooms and furnishings. When accommodation is reserved for you (by a travel agent, *Office de Tourisme* representative at the airport, etc.) this risk is hard to avoid. If the visitor does his own searching, the best procedure is to see the room before filling out the reservation form.

In principle, a hotel located in one of the downtown *quartiers* is a good choice due to the proximity and accessibility to sites and places of entertainment. When reserving from out of Paris, ask for a hotel in Quartiers 1-6.

In the list of hotels below, there are two criteria over and above the star rating. In the 4-star deluxe and 4-star categories, the hotels have been listed because they are the best known, good classic hotels. They are expensive, but you can rest assured that all your needs will be catered to. In contrast, in the 1 to 3-star categories, we have selected those hotels that offer good accommodations at a relatively lower cost. It is recommended that you first try these when making your reservations, before looking elsewhere.

4-star deluxe hotels
Claridge-Bellman: 37 rue François 1er, 8e, tel. 47.23.54.42. Franklin D. Roosevelt metro station. 42 rooms.
George V: 31 Av. George V, 8e, tel. 47.23.54.00. George V metro station. 292 rooms.
Holiday Inn: 10 Place de la République, 11e, tel. 43.55.33.34. République metro station. 333 rooms.

Le Bristol: 112 rue du Fg. Saint-Honoré, 8e, tel. 42.66.91.45. Champs Elysées-Clémenceau metro station. 200 rooms.
L'hôtel Guy-Louis-Doboucheron: 13 rue des Beaux-Arts, 6e, tel. 43.25.27.22. Saint-Germain-des-Prés metro station. 27 rooms.
Meurice: 228 rue de Rivoli, 1er, tel. 42.60.38.60. Tuileries metro station. 187 rooms.
Plaza-Athénée: 25 Av. Montaigne, 8e, tel. 47.23.78.33. Franklin D. Roosevelt metro station. 219 rooms.
Raphaël: 17 Av. Kléber, 16e, tel. 45.02.16.00. Kléber metro station. 89 rooms.
Ritz: 15 Place Vendôme, 1er, tel. 42.60.38.30. Opéra metro station. 184 rooms.

4-star hotels
Prices range from 700-1500f for a single, 900-1800f for a double.
Alexander: 102 Av. Victor Hugo, 16e tel. 45.53.64.65. Victor Hugo metro station. 62 rooms.
Castiglione: 40 rue du Fg. Saint-Honoré, 8e, tel. 42.65.07.50. Concorde metro station. 149 rooms.
Edouard VII: 39 Av. de L'Opéra, 2e, tel. 42.61.56.90. Opéra metro station. 100 rooms.
Hilton International Paris: 18 Av. de Suffren, 15e, tel. 42.73.92.00. Sèvres Lecourbe metro station. 456 rooms.
Madeleine Palace: 8 rue Cambon, 1er, tel. 42.60.37.82. Concorde metro station. 94 rooms.
Pavillon de la Reine: 28 Place des Vosges, 3e, tel. 42.77.96.40. Chemin-Vert metro station. 53 rooms.
Queen-Elizabeth: 41 Av. Pierre, 1er de Sebrie, 8e, tel. 47.20.80.56. Concorde metro station. 67 rooms.
Réginal: 2 Place des Pyramides, 1er, tel. 42.60.31.10. Tuileries metro station. 130 rooms.
Westminster: 13 rue de la Paix, 2e, tel. 42.61.57.46. Opéra metro station. 102 rooms.

3-star hotels
Prices range from 300-500f for a single,350-600f for a double.
Agora St-Germain: 42 rue des Bernadins, 5e, tel. 46.34.13.00. Mauber-Mutualité metro station. 39 rooms.
De L'Abbaye Saint-Germain: 10 rue Cassette, 6e, tel. 45.44.38.11. Saint-Sulpice metro station. 43 rooms.
De la Bretonnerie: 22 rue St.-Croix-de-la-Bretonnerie, 4e, tel. 48.87.77.63. Hôtel de Ville metro station. 32 rooms.
Du Pas de Calais: 59 rue des Saint-Pères, 6e, tel. 45.48.78.74. Saint-Germain-des-Prés metro station.

Elysa Luxembourg: 6 rue Gay Lussac, 5e, tel. 43.25.31.74. Luxembourg metro station. 30 rooms.
Le Loiret: 5 rue des Bons-Enfants, 1er, tel. 42.96.34.34. Châtelet metro station. 31 rooms.
Louvre Forum: 25 rue du Bouloi, 1er, tel. 42.36.54.19. Louvre metro station. 28 rooms.
Madison Elysées: 54 rue Galile, 8e, tel. 47.20.70.47. George V metro station. 26 rooms.
Saint-Germain-des-Prés: 36 rue Bonaparte, 6e, tel. 43.26.00.19. Saint-Germain-des-Prés metro station. 30 rooms.
Saint Merry: 78 rue de la Verrerie, 4e, tel. 42.78.14.15. Hôtel de Ville metro station. 12 rooms.
Saint-Petersbourg: 33 rue Caumartin, 9e, tel. 42.66.60.38. Opéra metro station. 120 rooms.
Sélect: 1 Place de la Sorbonne, 5e, tel. 46.34.14.80. Saint-Michel metro station. 69 rooms.

2-star hotels

Price ranges from 220-380f for a single, 250-400f for a double.
Bellevue et Chariot d'Or: 39 rue de Turbigo, 3e, tel. 48.87.45.60. Réaumur-Sebastopol metro station. 59 rooms.
D'Albe: 1 rue de la Harpe, 5e, tel. 46.34.09.70. Saint-Michel metro station. 43 rooms.
De La Madeleine: rue de Surène, 8e, tel. 42.65.71.61. Madeleine metro station. 30 rooms.
De La Sorbonne: 6 rue Victor Cousin, 5e, tel. 43.54.58.08. Odéon metro station. 37 rooms.
De Nice: 155 bd. de Montparnasse, 6e, tel. 43.26.60.24. Raspail metro station. 26 rooms.
Familia: 11 rue des Ecoles, 5e, tel. 43.54.55.27. Jussieu metro station. 30 rooms.
Moderne hôtel Montogolfier: 6 rue Montgolfier, 3e, tel. 42.77.17.61. Arts et Métiers metro station. 30 rooms.
Molière: 14 rue de Vaugirard, 6e, tel. 46.34.18.50. Odéon metro station. 15 rooms.
Saint-Germain: 88 rue du Bac, 7e tel. 45.48.62.92. Bac metro station. 29 rooms.
Studio Hôtel: 4 rue de Vieux Colombier, 6e, tel. 45.48.31.81. Saint-Sulpice metro station. 34 rooms.
Royal Park: 5 rue Castellane, 8e, tel. 42.66.14.44. Madeleine metro station. 30 rooms.
Washington Opéra: 50 rue de Richelieu, 1er, tel. 42.96.68.06. Palais-Royal metro station. 35 rooms.

1-star hotels

Prices range from 100f-260f for a single, 120-280f for a double.

Austins Hôtel: 26 rue d'Amsterdam, 9e, tel. 48.74.48.71. Saint-Lazare metro station. 32 rooms.

De la Herse d'Or: 29 rue Saint-Antoine, 4e, tel. 48.87.84.09. Bastille metro sation. 36 rooms.

De La Paix: 19 rue du Gros-Caillou, 7e, tel. 45.51.86.17. Ecole Militaire metro station. 23 rooms.

De Rouen: 42 rue Croix des Petits Champs, 1er, tel. 42.61.38.21. Les Halles metro station. 27 rooms.

Grand Hôtel de Besanon: 56 rue Montorgeuil, 2e, tel. 42.36.41.08. Les Halles metro station. 27 rooms.

Grand Hôtel Jeanne d'Arc: 3 rue Jarente, 4e, tel. 48.87.62.11. Saint-Paul metro station. 39 rooms.

Grand Hôtel Saint-Michel: 19 rue de Cujas, 5e, tel. 46.33.33.02. Odéon metro station. 67 rooms.

Haussmann: 89 rue de Provence, 9e, tel. 48.74.24.57. Saint-Lazare metro station. 31 rooms.

Richelieu Mazarin: 51 rue de Richelieu, 1er, tel. 42.37.46.20. Palais-Royal metro station. 14 rooms.

Tiquetonne: 6 rue Tiquetonne, 2e, tel. 42.36.94.58. Etienne Marcel metro station. 47 rooms.

Paris also has some 12,000 beds for young travelers. For information and direction, contact:

AJF: 12 rue des Barres, 4e, tel. 42.72.72.09. Hôtel de Ville metro station.

UCRIF: 20 rue Jean Jacques Rousseau, 1er, tel. 42.36.88.18. Les Halles metro station.

The Paris Youth Hostel: 8 Bd Jules Ferry, 11e, tel. 43.57.55.60. République metro station.

You may also rent a room or flat by the week or month. Prices vary widely. Make inquiries at one of the following:

Arcotle Tour le Tolem: 57-59 Quai de Grenelle, 15e, tel. 40.43.79.45. Bir-Hakeim metro station.

Club Expo: 20 rue Oradour-sur-Glane, 15e, tel. 45.54.97.43. Porte de Versailles metro station.

Résidence la Fontaine: 2 rue St.-Lazare, 9e, tel. 48.78.32.86. St.-Lazare metro station.

Those who prefer to rough it are welcome to combine a tour of Paris with accommodation in a tent. A campground in the Boulogne forest offers tent surfaces, power outlets and showers: *Camping Bois de Boulogne*, Route du Bord de l'Eau, tel. 45.06.14.98. or 45.24.30.00. Porte Maillot metro station. Open all year round, very crowded during July and August. Transportation from the metro station is available April-Sept.

Some Parisians rent out rooms to tourists. The Paris Tourist Office has lists of hundreds of such offers. Contact them for information at 127 av. des Champs Elysées, 8e, tel. 47.23.61.72. Etoile metro station.

Practical tips for getting around

Currency

The French currency is **le franc**, divided into 100 **centime**. It is customarily abbreviated f or ff (Franc Français), together with c for centimes. Coins and banknotes in circulation are 5c, 10c, 20c, 50c, 1f, 20f, 50f, 100f, 200f, 500f.

There is no legal limit to the amount of money tourists may bring into the country. When leaving the country, however, one is limited to taking 5,000f in French currency.

All international credit cards are honored in France, but not in equal measure everywhere. Some places accept all, others some, a few none at all. The most frequently honored cards are *Visa*, which is known as *Carte Bleue*, "the blue card", and *Eurocard*. If you lose credit cards, call one of the following numbers immediately: *Visa*: tel. 43.23.46.46 and *Diners Club*: tel. 47.62.75.00.

Traveler's checks are gladly accepted in most establishments and are easily cashed for francs in the bank. In general, it is worthwhile to arrive in France with French money or franc-denominated traveler's checks, as you are not charged commission when cashing these. If that cannot be arranged, change money in a bank. Private moneychangers charge higher commissions, and hotels sometimes offer exchange rates substantially lower than the official rate.

Communication

Paris has some 7,000 public telephones (many out of order) and 163 post offices. Until a few years ago, most of the public telephone boxes were coin operated. These were constantly broken into to steal the money, or vandalized by those using various methods to get free calls. Consequently, a solution to the problem was found whereby the majority of public phones are now operated by a magnetic card which can be purchased from the post office or the *Tabac* counter of most coffee shops. The price of a 50-call card is 40f, and a 120-call card costs 96f. Ask for a *Télé-Carte.*

Follow these steps when using the card:
Lift the receiver.
Insert the magnetic card in the direction indicated by the arrow.
Close the metal "curtain".
Wait for the number of unused calls still available on the card to appear on the screen.
Dial. (The dialed number will appear on the screen.)
At the end of the call, replace the receiver and open the metal "curtain" to retrieve the card.

Post offices are open weekdays 8am-7pm, Sat. 8am-noon, closed Sun. The central post office — 52 rue du Louvre, 1er (Louvre metro station) — is open day and night for telephone and telegraph service.

Stamps are sold at all post offices, as well as at *Tabac* stands. They are sometimes available at hotel reception desks.

Telegrams may be sent by phone:
In English: tel. 42.33.21.11.
In French: tel. 44.41.11.11.
In other languages: tel. 42.33.44.11.

Telex messages may be sent from 7 rue Feyedeau, 2^{e}; Bourse metro station. Open daily from 8am-11:30pm.

Banks

Central banks and their branches are open daily, 9am-4:30pm, closed Sat. and Sun. Moneychangers at airports and at major metro stations are open until late and on weekends.

Gare D'Austerlitz (until 9pm): tel. 45.84.91.40.
Gare de Lyon (until 11pm): tel. 43.41.52.70.
Gare de L'Est (until 9pm): tel. 42.06.51.97.
Gare St.-Lazare (until 9pm): tel. 43.87.72.51.
Gare du Nord (until 10pm): tel. 42.80.11.50.
Charles de Gaulle: (6am-11:30pm).
Orly: (6am-11:30pm).

Shopping

Paris' large department stores are open daily 9:30am-6:30pm, closed Sun. Some are open until 10pm one day per week (no fixed day).

Shops usually open around 10am and close at 7pm. Some take a one or two hour siesta at noon or 1pm. Shops are closed Sunday and, in some cases, Monday. Note that quite a few shops close in August for *vacances*, the annual vacation. Department stores stay open.

We survey the department stores and many smaller shops in "Filling the Basket".

Special business services

Service 2A at Charles de Gaule and Orly Airports enable businesspeople to obtain information and arrange office services immediately upon arrival: tel. 48.62.22.90

The address for information and help in organizing business exhibitions or meetings is *Le Comité Parisien de Congrès, Bureau des Congrès de l'Office de Tourisme* de Paris. It is located at 127 Champs-Elysées, 8e, tel. 47.20.12.55. or 47.23.61.72: Telex 611984 SIP PARIS.

Information on international, commercial or professional expositions: tel. 45.00.38.63. or 47.55.99.12.

Chauffeured car rental: Paris, 25 rue d'Astorg, 8e, tel. 42.65.54.20. telex 650265.

Electricity

Voltage in Paris is 220V. Electric shavers and similar appliances which are designed for this voltage, work with no difficulty. When purchasing electrical items as gifts, check the standard to see that it suits the one you require.

Tipping

Tipping (*pourboire*, or "drinking money"), is not obligatory, of course. However, it has become part of the game in some fields of life in Paris, and avoiding it may make things unpleasant at times. For good and pleasant service, it is customary to tip taxi drivers 10% of the meter reading, usually 3-4f. Ushers in concerts, theaters or cinemas (one is always ushered) get 2-3f. Waiters in restaurants and cafes are tipped 10-15% of the bill. Tour guides, museum guides, etc. are given approx. 5f.

INTRODUCTION

General Remarks

Vagrants and drunks on the street or in the metro can be bothersome at times. Usually they want money and sometimes they try to frighten you. Ignore them and distance yourself from them as much as possible.

"Client hunters" take up position at the entrances of certain clubs, exclusive shops and even restaurants (especially in the Latin Quarter). They do not hesitate to take you by the arm and try to pull you in gently. Shake your head firmly and keep walking.

In metro passageways, particularly late at night and in remote stations, keep an eye open. Try to stay in a group of people and remain alert, though not frantic. Violence has been known to occur in the metro but proper caution is a good deterrent.

On the metro itself, be extremely wary of pickpockets and purse snatchers, especially at rush hour. The metro management gives the following advice:

Try not to carry large sums of money in your pockets.
Don't let any money show from your pockets.
Try not to keep money or valuables in outer pockets.
Try to have an inner pocket with a zipper or a-button.
Handbags with shoulder straps should be held under one's arm.
While seated, place handbags on your lap, not beside you.

PARIS

Getting To Know The City

Group Tours

The ability or desire to explore a strange city alone is individual. Many people prefer organized tours at one level or another, if only for initial orientation. An overview of the possibilities of organized sightseeing in Paris follows.

Sightseeing buses

Two companies offer a variety of tours around town in impressive fleets of buses (including double-deckers) with panoramic windows. There is no great difference between the companies, neither in the content of the tours nor in the price:

Cityrama: 4 Place de Pyramides, 1er, tel. 42.60.30.14; Pyramides metro station.

Paris-Vision: 214 rue de Rivoli, 1er, tel. 42.60.31.25; Tuileries metro station.

Sample tours include: A 2-hour outing, no stops, including the following sights: Concorde, Notre-Dame, Bastille, Luxembourg, Invalides, Eiffel Tower, Arc de Triomphe, Sacré-Cœur, Opéra, Rivoli, Palais des Pyramides. Price: approx. 100f per person. These tours are good for a first impression of the city, and to help in your orientation during the walking tours. They are also suitable for those who only have a few hours in Paris and who want to have a quick overall glimpse of the city.

A **Paris Art-Tour**, provides a quick impression of some of the more famous art works in the city. The tour takes about three-and-a-half hours, and includes Notre Dame and the Louvre. The (possible) advantage of the tour is that it takes one directly to the *Mona Lisa*, without having to waste time looking for it or waiting in lines. The price is about 200f.

A **night-time excursion** takes you along the main streets and to various sites, snaking through heavy traffic. Price:

approx. 120f per person. There are a number of night-time excursions which include dinner and a night club show at one of the city's more famous hot spots (*Lido, Moulin Rouge, Crazy Horse,* etc.). The price per person is between 500-700f.

A **full-day outing** with a tour of the city and a side trip to Versailles. Price: approx. 330f per person including one meal. A more thorough tour is devoted exclusively to the Palace of Versailles and its gardens. 9:30am-4:15pm. Price: approx. 280f per person (not including lunch).

A full-day outing to the more remote castles in the Loire Valley. 7:15am-8:00pm. Price: approx. 650f per person (including lunch).

A longer and more distant outing is a **two-day tour** which includes the Loire Valley and St-Michel mountain (famous for, among other things, the tide turning it into an island). The guided tour, including meals and lodging in a 3-star hotel costs about 1700f per person.

Brochures are available at every tourist site, hotel and airport. Reception clerks can place reservations; alternatively, call the company offices. Prices often include transportation from your hotel and back.

Sightseeing boats

The view from the deck of a boat on the Seine offers a beautiful, interesting and educational look at Paris. This highly popular excursion combines the pleasure of a cruise with the beauty of the bridges and sites along the route. Several examples of cruise companies and recommended itineraries follow.

Les Bateaux Mouches: Pont de l'Alma, 8^{e}, tel. 42.25.96.10, 42.25.22.55 or 43.59.30.30; Alma Marceau metro station. The cruise takes about 1 1/4 hours; inquire by telephone for departure times. Price: 30f per person. A cruise which includes lunch on board costs 300f. For a festive cruise dinner, the price is 500f (jacket and tie required).

Vedettes de Paris Ile de France: Pont d'Iéna, 7e, tel. 45.05.71.29; Bir-Hakeim metro station (near the Eiffel Tower). The tour takes about 1 hour, and leaves every 30 minutes. From May-October,there are night tours, starting from 9pm.

Price: 30f per person; 15f for children under 10.

Les Vedettes du Pont Neuf: Square du Vert Galant, 1er, tel. 46.33.98.38; Pont Neuf metro station. 1 hour cruise; inquire by phone for departure times. Price: 25f per person, 12f for children under 10. There are night tours every evening from April-October, starting at 9pm. Price: 30f.

Le Canal Saint-Martin: This canal dates back to the time when cargo barges brought merchandise and raw materials into the city, doing the work of today's trucks. The canal begins near **Place de République** in Quartier 10, near rue Leon Jouhaux, and continues north towards **Place Stalingrad** on the outskirts of Quartier 19. The canal joins up with other canals and ultimately with the Seine. The tour along the canal is interesting, and is a reminder of the industrial revolution which took place in the 19th century. Along the way one can see "antique" locks used for lowering and raising the water level. One can either walk along the canal by foot (which is free!) or take a cruise on the Seine and along the canal. There are two daily cruises. In the morning it leaves from Quai Anatole-France, Solférino metro station, while in the afternoon it goes in the opposite direction, departing from La Villette, Porte de Pantin metro station. The trip takes about half a day. Price: 90f, 50f for children. Regular tours from April-November, advance booking essential, tel.42.40.96.97. The rest of the year it is possible to join groups which have arranged private cruises by calling this same number.

Sightseeing helicopters and airplanes

Visitors with limited time — or who favor a bird's eye view — will appreciate the following options:

Hélifrance offers a variety of helicopter tours. It is located at the Paris helicopter airport, at 4 av. de la Porte de Sèvres in Quartier 15, Balard metro station. Tel. 45.54.95.11. The following prices should give you a good indication as to what is available:

A trip over La Défense — 215f.
A flight around Versailles — 320f.
A comprehensive flight above Paris — 530f.
A trip including all of the above sights, taking about half an hour — 800f.

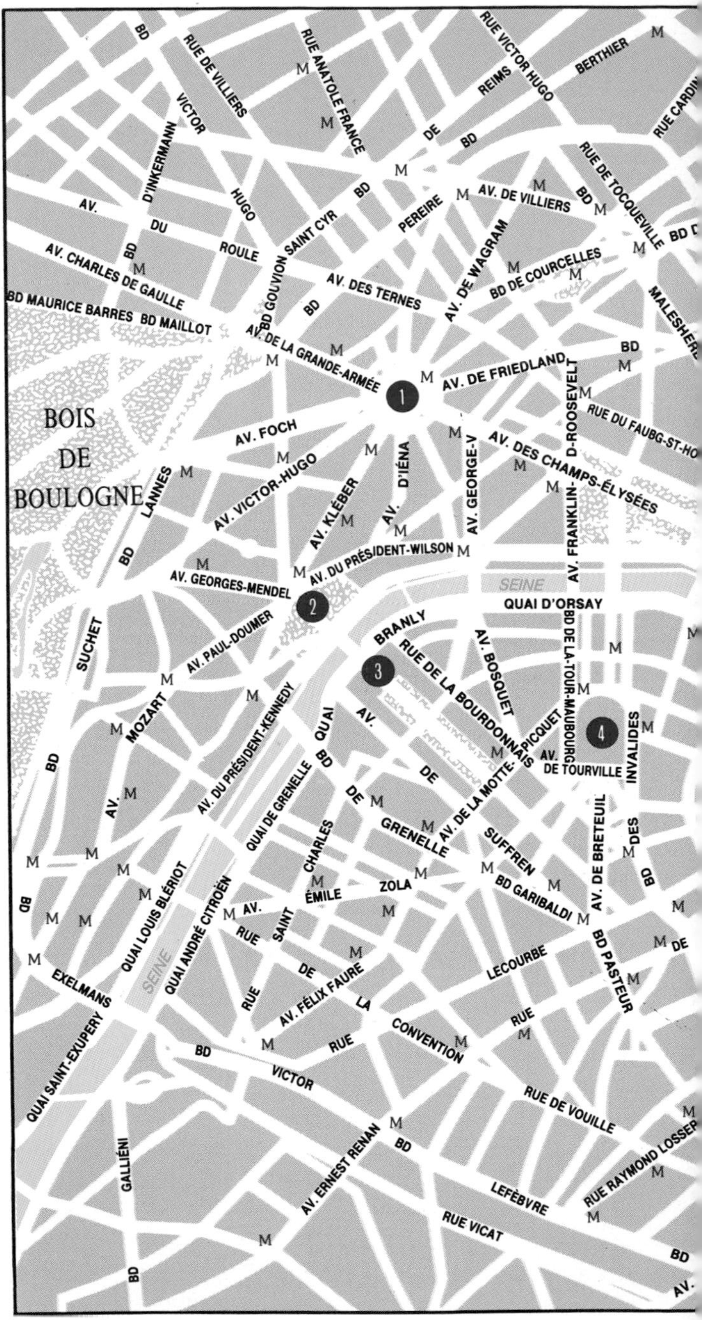
BOIS
DE
BOULOGNE
RUE DE VILLIERS
RUE ANATOLE FRANCE
RUE VICTOR HUGO
REIMS
BERTHIER
RUE CARDIN
VICTOR
HUGO
D'INKERMANN
AV.
DU
ROULE
BD GOUVION SAINT CYR
BD
PEREIRE
DE
AV. DE VILLIERS
RUE DE TOCQUEVILLE
BD
AV. CHARLES DE GAULLE
BD MAURICE BARRES
BD MAILLOT
AV. DES TERNES
AV. DE WAGRAM
BD DE COURCELLES
MALESHERB
AV. DE LA GRANDE-ARMÉE
AV. DE FRIEDLAND
AV. FRANKLIN-D-ROOSEVELT
RUE DU FAUBG-ST-HO
AV. FOCH
AV. VICTOR-HUGO
AV. D'IÉNA
AV. GEORGE-V
AV. DES CHAMPS-ÉLYSÉES
LANNES
AV. KLÉBER
AV. DU PRÉSIDENT-WILSON
AV. GEORGES-MENDEL
SEINE
QUAI D'ORSAY
SUCHET
AV. PAUL-DOUMER
BRANLY
RUE DE LA BOURDONNAIS
AV. BOSQUET
BD DE LA-TOUR-MAUBOURG
MOZART
AV. DU PRÉSIDENT-KENNEDY
QUAI
AV.
PICQUET
AV. DE TOURVILLE
INVALIDES
QUAI DE GRENELLE
BD DE GRENELLE
DE
SUFFREN
AV. DE LA MOTTE-
AV. DE BRETEUIL
DES
CHARLES
ÉMILE
ZOLA
BD GARIBALDI
QUAI LOUIS BLÉRIOT
QUAI ANDRÉ CITROËN
AV.
RUE
SAINT
BD PASTEUR
LECOURBE
DE
EXELMANS
SEINE
RUE
AV. FÉLIX FAURE
LA
CONVENTION
RUE
QUAI SAINT-EXUPERY
BD
RUE
VICTOR
RUE DE VOUILLE
GALLIÉNI
AV. ERNEST RENAN
BD
LEFÈBVRE
RUE RAYMOND LOSSER
RUE VICAT
BD
AV.
1
2
3
4

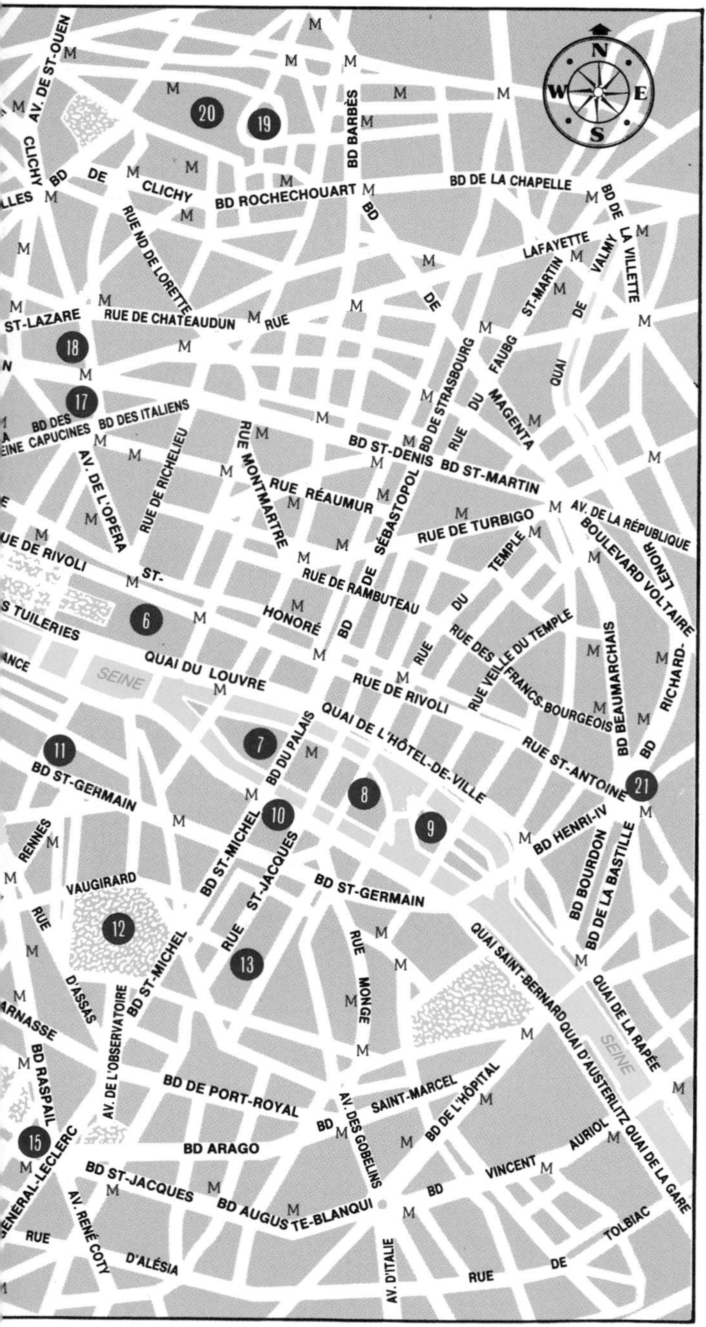
N
E
S
W
AV. DE ST-OUEN
CLICHY
LLES
BD DE CLICHY
RUE ND DE LORETTE
BD ROCHECHOUART
BD BARBÈS
BD DE LA CHAPELLE
BD DE LA VILLETTE
LAFAYETTE
ST-MARTIN
QUAI DE VALMY
RUE DE
FAUBG
ST-LAZARE
RUE DE CHATEAUDUN
RUE
BD DES CAPUCINES
BD DES ITALIENS
AV. DE L'OPERA
RUE DE RICHELIEU
RUE MONTMARTRE
BD ST-DENIS
BD DE STRASBOURG
RUE DU
MAGENTA
BD ST-MARTIN
RUE RÉAUMUR
BD DE SÉBASTOPOL
RUE DE TURBIGO
AV. DE LA RÉPUBLIQUE
BOULEVARD VOLTAIRE
LENOIR
RUE DU TEMPLE
RUE DE RIVOLI
ST-
HONORÉ
RUE DE RAMBUTEAU
TUILERIES
QUAI DU LOUVRE
SEINE
RUE DES FRANCS-BOURGEOIS
RUE VEILLE DU TEMPLE
BD BEAUMARCHAIS
BD RICHARD-
RUE DE RIVOLI
QUAI DE L'HÔTEL-DE-VILLE
BD DU PALAIS
RUE ST-ANTOINE
BD ST-GERMAIN
BD ST-MICHEL
RUE ST-JACQUES
BD HENRI-IV
BD BOURDON
BD DE LA BASTILLE
RENNES
VAUGIRARD
RUE
BD ST-GERMAIN
BD ST-MICHEL
RUE MONGE
QUAI SAINT-BERNARD
D'ASSAS
ARNASSE
AV. DE L'OBSERVATOIRE
QUAI DE LA RAPÉE
SEINE
QUAI D'AUSTERLITZ
BD RASPAIL
BD DE PORT-ROYAL
SAINT-MARCEL
BD
BD DE L'HÔPITAL
AV. DES GOBELINS
AURIOL
QUAI DE LA GARE
BD ARAGO
VINCENT
BD
BD ST-JACQUES
BD AUGUSTE-BLANQUI
GENERAL-LECLERC
AV. RENÉ COTY
RUE
D'ALÉSIA
AV. D'ITALIE
RUE DE TOLBIAC
20
19
18
17
6
7
8
9
10
11
12
13
15
21

Espace Plus also offers aerial tours of the city, but in a less conventional mode of transport — in a hot-air balloon! For those who enjoy adventure, you can book or obtain information from Tel. 46.05.91.25.

Index

1. Arc de Triomphe
2. Palais de Chaillot
3. Eiffel Tower
4. Les Invalides
5. Place de la Concorde
6. The Louvre
7. Ile de la Cité
8. Notre-Dame-de-Paris
9. Ile St-Louis
10. Latin Quarter
11. St-Germain-des-Prés
12. Luxembourg Gardens
13. The Panthéon
14. Montparnasse Tower
15. Place Denfert-Rochereau
16. Eglise de la Madeleine
17. Paris Opera House
18. Galeries Lafayette
19. Sacré-Cœur
20. Montmartre
21. Place de la Bastille

Exploring Paris and the Vicinity

Paris presents the visitor with an eclectic jumble of "musts", "shoulds", and "recommendeds". The systematic survey in the coming pages sorts them into several tour routes and provides, as far as is possible, thorough coverage of the city. When done on foot, which is the recommended way, they cover wide parts of the city in the most comprehensive manner.

Each route stops at museums, monuments, palaces, street landmarks, unusual shops, etc. They also include restaurants or places when one can have a light meals during the tour. Each begins with an introductory overview, enabling you to focus on the sites you personally find interesting and attractive. The selection of a wide variety of themes and sites along each route is deliberate. Once done, the visitor should come away feeling very familiar with the area. Each tourist may build a personalized tour from the thorough and detailed spectrum of possibilities provided. Each tour is accompanied by a map, specifying the recommended route and the precise location of the major sites.

The routes are designed to be covered on foot in one average touring day. The pace, of course, depends totally on one's capacity and the time one wishes to spend at each site.

There is also a list of additional sites attached to each route. These are lower priority attractions located not far from the route of your visit. Select those which are of interest to you.

Metro stations and bus stops at the point of departure are noted at the beginning of each tour.

Personal priorities, interests and schedules aside, certain attractions in Paris are genuine "musts" which no tourist can conceivably overlook. These are listed at the end of the guide.

The routes first cover the central *quartiers* of Paris, heading from downtown toward the fringes of the city. They then venture out a little — to the flea markets, the forests and gardens, Versailles, and... tomorrow's Paris. The last route embraces ultramodern and futuristic sites. These are the most innovative projects in Paris, projects which, by their very inception, make Paris what it is.

After touring the city itself, it is time to head for its hinterland. A chain of interesting cities surround Paris, notable for their special beauty, grace and grandeur. They offer the tourist a variety of interesting attractions, good restaurants and anything else a tourist might want. Day visits to these are definitely recommended.

Something a visitor to Paris must keep in mind is that the museums here are enormously popular attractions. The lines, which often stretch from the ticket booths right out into the street, can sometimes cause one to despair.

The number of people who visited the various museums in 1987 gives you some idea of the lines that one encounters. For example, 7,225,000 people visited the Pompidou Center in the course of the year! This is the record, but the other figures are hardly negligible either: La Villette — 2,725,000, the Louvre — 2,575,000 (less than the previous year) and d'Orsay — 2,575,000. Incidentally, 70% of these are tourists.

The solution is to arrive early in the morning, and wait patiently. Of course, if you wish to avoid the crowds, it is best to visit during the winter.

The Seine River

The Royal Heart of Paris

Le Quartier Premier is the center of Paris, housing the Palais Royal, Palais du Louvre (with its museum), the Comedie Francaise Theater, and the Arc de Triomphe du Carrousel, a smaller version of the more famous Arc de Triomphe. To reach the area, take the metro to the Louvre or the Palais Royal station or buses 21, 74,76 or 81.

A quadrangle about 1,640 yards (1,500 m) long is formed by **Palais de Louvre**, the **Jardin des Tuileries** and **Place de la Concorde**. On one side of the quadrangle is the Seine River and on the other rue de Rivoli. In terms of population (a mere 19,000), this is the smallest *quartier* in Paris. Most buildings here are government offices, public institutions, opulent hotels (*Ritz*, *Inter-Continental*) and prestige shops (on rues de Rivoli and St.-Honoré).

Le Musée du Louvre — "The Louvre"

Open daily, 9:45am-5:15pm; closed Tues. Several exhibition halls open until 6:30pm, tel. 42.60.39.26. Sundays admission is free (but it is very crowded). The Louvre has six wings: Paintings and Drawings, Antiquities of the Ancient East, Sculpture, Egyptian Antiquities, Greek and Roman Antiquities, and *Objets d'Art*. This is in addition to temporary exhibits.

The Louvre is one of the largest and most famous museums in the world today, but that is not how it began. The palace, in its various forms, served for centuries as the residence of many of the kings of France.

The Louvre was originally built by Philip Augustus as a military bastion in 1200. In the 14th century, Charles V made it his home. François I completed the building and turned it into a grand palace. The Renaissance-style southwestern wing of the inner court (**La Cour Carrée**) survives from this period and is the oldest relic in the chain of structures visible today. Louis XIII enlarged and expanded the western wing of the inner court in a similar style and it was finally completed by Louis XIV. To the west, two wings branch out toward **Jardin**

des Tuileries. They date from the period of the Second Empire in the 19th century, during the reign of Napoleon III.

The Louvre Museum was opened to the public as a repository of *objets d'art* in 1795 with a collection begun by François I. His successors, particularly Louis XIV and Napoleon I, augmented and expanded it.

The next memorable person to make a contribution to the Louvre is President François Mitterand, who in 1981 gave the go-ahead for an ambitious project known as "Grande Louvre". As part of this scheme, the museum is currently undergoing vast changes.

Initially, it was decided to push out the offices of the Ministry of Finance which were located in the northern Richelieu wing. They have now been moved to the new complex built for them in Bercy. The vacated area has added more space to display many works which were previously kept in storage due to lack of space. This significant addition (which adds 25,000 sq. m floor space to the existing 30,000 sq. m.) is expected to be completed by the mid-1990s in time for the celebrations commerating 200 years since the museum's opening. These festivities will mark the completion of the "Grande Louvre" project.

Several of the alterations have already been completed. The entrance to the museum is now through a large glass pyramid, which was erected in the middle of "Napoléon's Courtyard". This design was chosen, on the suggestion of the Sino-American architect, Pei, as it does not compete with the style of the palace which surrounds it on three sides. A further three smaller pyramids were built alongside the large one, at a cost of one million francs. These, too, are constructed of glass and contain pools of water with fountains.

The main pyramid, which stands some 65 ft. (20 m) high, covers the new underground entrance level of the museum. The fact that it was built of glass, allows the sun to penetrate and illuminate the inner space. On entering via the pyramid an escalator brings you to the huge lobby which houses the ticket booths, information counters, orientation tables (which facilitate in locating any wing or section of the museum), a restaurant and a museum store which stocks books and other publications.

From the lobby, you also have access to the historical

THE ROYAL HEART AND ST-GERMAIN

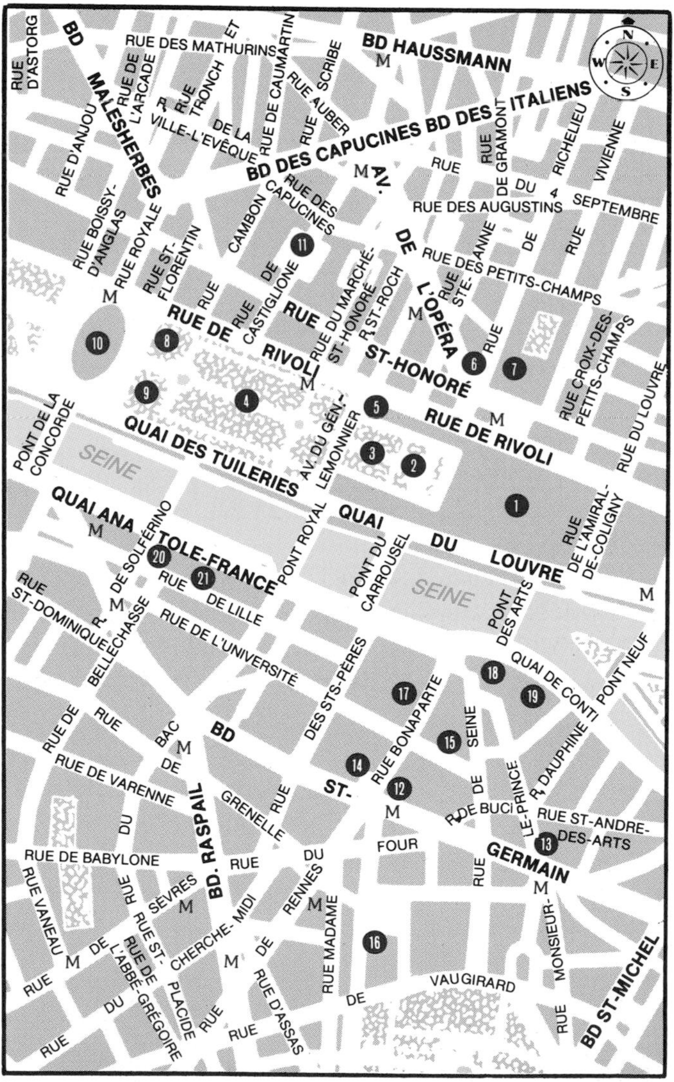

The Glass Pyramid — Entrance to the Louvre

foundations of palace. The extensive diggings here have revealed unparalleled archeological treasures. Initial figures record over 20,000 findings, including household utensils, various tools, *objets d'art* and jewelry, mainly from the Middle-Ages. Perhaps the most impressive discoveries made during the diggings were the fortress tower of King Philip-Augustus and the courtroom of King Louis the Holy, who reigned in the 13th century.

This new entrance level also houses halls for changing exhibits, which will be used to display items which until now

Index

1. The Louvre
2. Glass Pyramid
3. L'Arc de Triomphe du Carrousel
4. Jardin des Tuileries
5. Musée des Arts Décoratifs (Museum of Decorative Arts)
6. Comédie Française
7. Palais Royal
8. Musée du Jeu de Paume
9. Musée de l'Orangerie
10. Place de la Concorde
11. Place Vendôme
12. Eglise St-Germain des Prés
13. Café Procope
14. Les Deux Magots
15. Musée Delacroix
16. Eglise St-Sulpice
17. Ecole des Beaux-Arts
18. Institut de France
19. Hôtel des Monnaies (Numismatic Museum)
20. Musée de la Légion d'Honneur
21. Musée d'Orsay

have not been available for public viewing due to lack of space.

Collections in the Louvre: The halls of the Louvre exhibit more than 250,000 objects! To devote a few minutes to each would require several years... A tourist on a quick stopover has time only for a general overview and a selection focusing on the works he likes best or "must" see (such as the *Mona Lisa*).

Paintings: True, the *Mona Lisa* is perhaps the crowning glory of the Louvre and its most famous work. It was donated to the Louvre by Francois I, who was Leonardo da Vinci's patron for several years. Francois paid the artist 4000 florins for *Mona Lisa*. Even this sum, stupendous for its time, did not meet the artist's conditions and the king acquired the masterpiece only after da Vinci's death. The Louvre houses another four works by da Vinci — the most magnificent collection of its kind anywhere: it includes *The Virgin of the Rocks* and *St. John the Baptist*.

Da Vinci shares the hall with other titans of the Italian Renaissance (Raphael and Titian) and giants of other periods: Giotto, Giorgione, Botticelli, Piero della Francesca, Fra Angelico, Giovanni Bellini, Tintoretto, and others. Most of the Italian works are to be found on the first floor in the Grande Galerie, Salle des Etats, Salle des Sept Chiminees and Aile de Flore.

Spanish art is represented by works of, among others, El Greco, Murillo, Goya, Rivera and Velazquez. Most of the Spanish works are exhibited in the Pavillon de Flore, which is in the corner, facing Jardin des Tuileries on the first floor.

Flemish art and painters of the Low Countries also contribute significantly to the Louvre. They include paintings by Rembrandt (such as his famous self-portrait), Hieronymus Bosch, Vermeer, Frans Hals, Jan Van Eyck, Van Dyck and an important collection of works by Rubens. Most of the Dutch and Flemish masters can be seen on the first floor in the Petits Cabinets and Petits Cabinets des Tuileries.

The greatest practitioners of French art receive highly conspicuous coverage in this wing of the Louvre. The best known of these are La Tour, Poussin, Watteau, Fragonard, David, Ingres, Courbet and Delacroix. These are concentrated on the first and second floors in the Salon

Carré, Salle Duchatel, Grande-Galerie, Salle Mollien, Salle Daru and Salle Denon.

The most significant exhibits among the German artists are those of Durer (including his famous self-portrait which dates back to the 15th century) and Holbein. Their works are exhibited in the Petits Cabinets on the first floor.

English art has not been overlooked, and the most prominent works are those of Reynolds and Gainsborough, which can be found in Hall 12, on the second floor.

Greek and Roman Antiquities: This breathtaking collection spans the Early Classical period to the end of the Roman Empire. Here, the *pièce de resistance* is the *Venus de Milo*, probably created in the 3rd century BC. *Venus* was rediscovered in 1820 by a peasant on the island of Milo. She symbolizes the ancient Greeks' admiration of beauty and physical perfection. Other works of renown on display here are the winged female of *Victory at Samothrace*, *Parthenon* sculptures of Phidias, and *Hera of Samos*. No less impressive are the Roman reproductions of Greek works, such as *The Cnidian Aphrodite* and the busts of Roman emperors such as Nero, Caligula, Adrianus and others.

A natural extension of the Greek and Roman antiquities, are exhibits from the Etruscan culture. This mysterious nation, who lived in the 6th century BC, left very little evidence of its past and way of life in Tuscany, Italy. In the Etruscan halls, you can see jewelry, statues and perhaps most impressive, the adorned sarcophagus of Servitri.

The Greek, Roman and Etruscan antiquities are exhibited in halls 1-25 on the ground floor and halls 241-253 on the first floor.

Egyptian Antiquities: Primarily thanks to the French scholar Jean François Champollion, one of the greatest Egyptologists ever and the man who deciphered the hieroglyphics code, the Louvre is graced with one of the world's most memorable collections of Egyptian antiquities. Champollion went to Egypt with a party of scholars in 1798, following the defeat of Napoleon, and came home with what proved to be the foundation of a great collection. His findings were augmented by later acquisitions, including sculptures, reliefs, sarcophagi, jewelry of Rameses II, the treasure of King Tutankhamen and Queen Nefertiti.

Among the more impressive Egyptian antiquities are: the Sphinx of Tunis, made of magnificent granite, dating back two millennia BC and the dagger of Gebel-el-Arak with scenes of war and hunting carved on its ivory butt (or handle). Most of the Egyptian antiquities are concentrated in exhibits in the south-west corner of the building in halls 125-135, on the ground floor, and on the first floor, in the same corner, in halls A-H.

Antiquities of the Ancient East: The collection begins with the original and universally famous Code of Hammurabi: a large tablet of basalt engraved with the 282 laws of the Babylonian king. His likeness, is engraved into a small stone positioned beside the codex in a display case.

This collection, originating mainly in Mesopotamia, is especially attractive to bibliophiles. It displays the stele of King Naram-Sin of the Accadian dynasty, statues of the goddess Astarte, the stele of Vultures, depicting one of the victories of King Shomer, of the third millenium BC, reliefs from the palace of King Assurbanipal who lived in the 7th century BC, and more. These exhibits can be seen in the north-east wing of the Louvre, halls I-XXII, on the ground floor.

Sculpture: The lavish collection spans the Middle Ages, the Renaissance and the modern era with masterpieces by Michelangelo (*The Slaves*), Cellini, Pilon, Mazzoni, Della Robbia and others. French sculpture over the ages is also copiously represented by Coustou, Robert, Henri Laurens, Bouchardon and others. These works of sculpture are to be found on the ground floor in the south-west wing, halls 1-28.

Objets d'art, **furnishings and antiquities:** One need not be an art lover to appreciate this collection. The many exhibits include a ring which belonged to St. Louis; the royal crowns of Louis XV and Napoleon; Cardinal Richelieu's desk and Charles X's diamond-studded sword. The "regent" is probably a 137-carat diamond discovered in India in the late 17th century and acquired by Crown Prince Philip d'Orléans in 1791, for the astronomical price (in any era) of 12 million francs. This rich and varied collection can be seen in halls 1-41 in the north-east wing on the first floor.

After having visited the Louvre, rest a bit and make acquaintance with one of Paris' best-known and most refined tea salons — *Angelina*, 226 rue de Rivoli, tel. 42.60.82.00. The teahouse, roughly in the middle of Jardin des Tuileries, across rue Rivoli which runs parallel to it to the north, is perhaps the loveliest example of turn-of-the-century Parisian leisure. Characteristics include marble columns, ornate carvings, Louis XV armchairs and pots of indescribably delicious hot chocolate with whipped cream. Then there's the house specialty: Mont Blanc cake — whipped cream, vanilla cream and chopped chestnuts. Coffee and cake about 40f per person. Open 9:30am-7pm; closed in August.

On rue de Rivoli, return to the Louvre, to the north-western arm of the palace where another interesting museum is located. The **Musée des Arts Décoratifs**, at 107 rue de Rivoli, 1er, tel. 42.60.32.14, is open daily from 11am-6pm. Closed Mon. and Tues. Entrance 20f.

After several years of extensive renovations, this important museum now provides a comprehensive look at the different sides of "practical art". On display are daily household articles, dating from the Middle Ages until the present day, showing man's development in thought, beauty and taste as perceived through these objects. Man has always used furniture, metal tools, carpets and *objects d'art* fashioned from glass and clay, but these have altered and undergone vast changes from period to period. In this museum one can trace the gradual differences and transformations of all these objects.

A fun exhibition (for both adults and children) also awaits one at this museum. Here one can see an impressive collection of toys dating from the 18th century to the present day. The museum also arranges a number of changing exhibitions.

Next to this museum is yet another, the **Musée des Arts de la Mode**, open the same hours as Musée des Arts Decoratifs, entrance 25f. It surveys the development of clothing, from the 18th century until today. The museum displays a tasteful and representative selection, from the vast collections at its disposal, which includes about 10,000 suits of clothing, as well as tens of thousands of individual garments and accessories.

Upon leaving the Louvre, head east between the two arms of the palace, to the **Arc de Triomphe du Carrousel**, the (relatively) little brother of the great Arc de Triomphe in Place d'Etoile-Charles de Gaulle. Completed in 1809, the arch commemorates Napoléon's great victories in 1805, including the Battle of Austerlitz.

The arch has beautiful pink marble columns. A view from the air or from a map, reveals the imaginary straight line between it and the great Arc at Place de l'Etoile, via the obelisk in Place de la Concorde.

Past the Arc de Triomphe du Carrousel is **Jardin des Tuileries**. It originally belonged to Palais des Tuileries which the Communards burned to the ground in 1871. Queen Catherine de Medici built the palace in the 16th century but never lived there. Her fortune teller told her that it was destined for chronic trouble. He was right. Revolutionaries trapped the royal family here in 1792 and members of the Royal Swiss Guard were massacred there the same year. (Those who have been to Lucern, Switzerland, will have seen the "Crying Lion" carved in their memory.) Charles X was forcibly expelled from this spot in 1830, as was Louis Philippe in 1848. Legend tells that the ghost of a red-faced man — one of Queen Catherine's victims — appeared in the garden every time a disaster occurred in Tuileries. Some Parisians add that the ghost had a satisfied look on his face at the sight of retribution visited on the kingdom which had claimed his life...

Today's visitor, by contrast, observes a wealth of statues of Greek and other gods and the sculpted likeness of Le Notre, Louis XIV's chief gardener, who gave Jardin des Tuileries its "French-style" design. In 1988, after a long dispute, an impressive statue of Alfred Dreyfus was placed in the garden. Dreyfus was the French army officer of Jewish extraction, who was convicted on a false charge of treason. This statue, by the famous caricaturist Tim, can be seen about midway down the garden, on the southern side.

A pair of structures face one another in the corners of the eastern end of the garden. The northern of these is **Musée Jeu de Paume**. The museum used to house an exceptional collection of works of the greatest Impressionist artists, but this has been moved to the Musée d'Orsay. Once the extensive renovations on the building have been completed, it will be used for temporary exhibitions of contemporary art.

Next to Musée Jeu de Paume, at the far end of Jardin des

Tuileries (near the Seine), **Musée de l'Orangerie** comes into view. Open daily 9:45am-5:15pm, closed Tues. Admission 15f. Here are several important examples of Impressionist art, including Claude Monet's *Water Lilies* and works by Modigliani, Matisse, Cezanne, Utrillo, Soutine, Rousseau and Picasso. Monet presented the *Water Lilies*, which are found on the ground floor, to the Government of France to commemorate the end of World War I in 1918, but insisted on improving the eight paintings until his death in 1926. They were first displayed to the public in 1927. Note: the hall in which they are displayed is usually closed every day between noon-2pm.

Hungry? Head north from rue de Rivoli, opposite from Musée Jeu de Paume, to rue Mondovi. The owners of *Lescure* claim that this pleasant restaurant, at 7 rue Mondevi, has been in operation and built a reputation at this site since 1919. It certainly exudes the charm of those by-gone days and offers a delicious and very generous bourgeois selection of attractive French dishes including excellent *bœuf bourguignon*. A set dinner will cost about 75f, while if you order à la carte it can jump up to about of 150f, but is still worthwhile. Open till 10pm, recommended for lunch or dinner, tel. 42.60.18.91.

The next stop is **Place de la Concorde**. Originally called Place Louis XV, it became Place de la Revolution in 1772 and Place de la Concorde (unity of hearts) in 1795. For a short period it glorified the name of Louis XVI, but since 1830, it has retained its present name.

Place de la Concorde is the largest and perhaps the most impressive plaza in Paris. From its center one can look west toward Champs-Elysées and the great Arc de Triomphe; south to Pont de la Concorde and beyond, Palais Bourbon (home of the National Assembly, France's Parliament), constructed in 1722 for the Duchess of Bourbon, daughter of Louis XIV, with the pillared facade added by Napoléon; east to Jardin des Tuileries and the Louvre; and north to La rue Royale, which ends at the Church of the Madeleine.

In the center of the plaza, during the Revolution, stood the dreaded guillotine. It lopped off more than a thousand heads, including those of such luminaries as Louis XVI, Marie Antoinette, Countess du Barry, Danton, and Robespierre.

Jardin des Tuileries — The Dreyfus statue

At the same spot today, the 3,300 year old **Obelisk of Luxor** soars 88.5 ft. (27 m) into the sky. The obelisk was presented to King Louis Philippe in 1836 by Muhammad Ali, ruler of Egypt. The square is also graced with two large fountains embellished with sculptured nymphs and gods who spill water endlessly into a pool. Another eight statues, one in each corner of the plaza, represent eight great cities in France: Brest, Rouen, Strasbourg, Lille, Nantes, Bordeaux, Marseilles and Lyon.

Courtyard of Palais Royal

Additional points of interest

North of Jardin des Tuileries, from rue de Rivoli, follow rue Castiglione to **Place Vendôme**. This is a prestigious area, home to quite a few opulent jewelry shops with "for display only" prices. In the center of the plaza stands a victory column. Erected in 1806, it was cast in bronze from 250 Austrian and Russian cannons captured by Napoleon's armies after the Battle of Austerlitz. The column was renovated in 1871.

House No. 12 on the plaza is **the last residence of Chopin**. No. 11 houses the **French Ministry of Justice**; No. 13 is the opulent *Hotel Ritz*.

Opposite the northern entrance to the Louvre is **Palais Royal**. Though it was built in the 17th century as Cardinal Richelieu's residence, much has happened here since that time. During the Revolution, it actually housed gaming halls and a brothel. Parts of it were torched in 1871, but were later restored. Today the palace gardens are a public park, while the southern section of the building houses the State Council and the Ministry of Culture. In the rear sections are luxury shops and apartments, including the houses where famous artists and authors, such as Cocteau and Collette, used to live. In the southern section of the park stand the striped pillars which were placed there in 1986. These modern "pyjama-clad" works of art prevented the construction of an underground parking garage and a rehearsal hall for La Comédie Française which were slated for this area.

Just west of Palais Royal is **La Comédie Française** at 2 rue de Richelieu. The theater, first established in 1680 by Louis XIV, has been located here since the late 1700s. The interior entrance is graced with a lovely sculpture of Voltaire by Houdon. It also displays the famous armchair in which Molière was sitting at the performance of *The Imaginary Invalid* on the night he fell ill and died. Today, the theater presents a classical French repertoire — Molière, Racine, Corneille, together with modern French and other dramas (information about performances, tel. 40.15.00.15; ticket prices: 40-140f).

St.-Germain — Intellectuals and Aristocracy

This tour covers much of *Quartier 6* and the northeastern corner of *Quartier 7*. It consists of two parts: St.-Germain and Faubourg (suburb) St.-Germain.

For centuries this area was somewhat detached from Paris proper, making its way alone. This separation was so obvious that the trouble was never taken to build a bridge across the Seine along this stretch. Transportation was by ferry (*bac*), opposite the street which is known today as rue du Bac.

It was Louis XIV, while expanding the Louvre, who had the first bridge, Pont Royal (Royal Bridge), built in order to speed up the transportation of construction stones across the river from the quarries in southern Paris.

The situation began to improve when, during the reign of Louis XV (mid-18th century), many court nobles in Versailles began migrating back toward Paris. Many of them chose the area now known as Faubourg St.-Germain as the site for their mansions. Many of these homes still survive, lending the area an elegant and impressive atmosphere.Note the Hôtel Matignon, the Prime Minister's official residence, 57 rue de Varenne, and Hôtel de Courteilles, the Ministry of Education, at 110 rue de Grenelle.

Additional palaces of French nobility, built in Louis XV style, can be seen on rue Lille and rue L'Université. Many are still occupied by descendants of the original owners, known today as old families. The area is also home to many foreign embassies, respectable institutions and government ministries (Agriculture, Transportation, Industry, Development and Energy).

To the east, around the church of St.-Germain-des-Prés, the area changes. The famous Ecole des Beaux Arts is north of the church and, to the east, are several of Paris' oldest and loveliest cafes. *Le Café Procope* (est. 1686), 13 rue de l'Ancienne Comédie, is considered the "old man" of Paris cafes and was the favorite of the heroes of the revolution, such as Danton and Robespierre, as well as famous personalities like Voltaire, Balzac and Anatole France. Today, you can get a fair meal, for about 200f per person.

Incidentally, the street, rue de l'Ancienne Comédie, acquired its name from La Comédie Française, the theater which was once located at No. 14.

The area hosts another cafe which has become an institution. It is *Les Deux Magots*, just off the plaza of Eglise de St.-Germain-des-Prés. A favorite among philosophers, authors, poets and artists, it was a regular long-time watering hole for Sartre and Simone de Beauvoir among others. Try it for breakfast or for a shot of one of the 25 superb brands of whisky at the bar.

Place Furstenberg, slightly northeast of the church, is one of the most charming plazas in Paris. In the evening, the lighting gives the plaza a surrealistic appearance. Alongside it is Musée Delacroix.

Musée Delacroix, 6 Place Furstenberg, commemorates Eugene Delacroix (1798-1863), one of the greatest French Romanticists, who spent his last years here. The residence-cum-museum is open daily 9:45am-5:45pm, closed Tues. Delacroix astounded his contemporaries with huge canvases depicting hunting scenes, battles and heroic postures. Today Delacroix's home and its studio are packed with documents, letters, pictures, memorabilia and paintings which recall his tempestuous life and art.

From St.-Germain, follow rue Bonaparte south to the large square lying in the shadow of the massive **Eglise St-Sulpice** which is 375 ft. (115 m) long and 185 ft. (56 m) wide. Construction on the church began in 1646, and continued under different architects for about one hundred years, with each adding a different style. Of particular interest is Delacroix's *Jacob's Struggle with the Angel*, which hangs inside the church.

This area, packed with history and beauty, deserves leisurely exploration. Notice the profusion of marble plaques on the building facades noting the important personages who once lived there. Rue de Rennes, which goes down in a southerly direction, to the Montparnasse Tower, is always bustling with shoppers.

Rue St. André des Arts, a bustling street running east from Eglise St.-Germain almost to Place St.-Michel, offers a pleasurable stroll amid alleyways, galleries and houses in "Old Paris" style.

To reach the area by metro, get off at St.-Sulpice, rue du Bac, St.-Germain-des-Prés or Mabillon; by bus, lines 39, 48, 63, 70, 86, 95 or 96.

L'Eglise de St.-Germain-des-Prés is open daily 7:30am-7:45pm; from 12:30pm on Monday.

The foundations of the church dated back to the 6th century AD, when King Childebert I of the Merovingian dynasty returned from a victorious campaign in Spain with two souvenirs: St. Vincent's habit and a golden cross which belonged to King Solomon. The church and the adjacent abbey were built to house these treasures. Subsequently expanded, the complex became a center of the Benedictine Order. It was enclosed by a wall and functioned as a burial ground for the Merovingian kings. To preserve their independence, the Benedictine monks cultivated fields, built barns and raised livestock around the monastery. Hence St.-Germain's suffix: *des prés*, French for "of the grazing ground". The church was razed to the ground twice during the Norman invasions, and the present structure dates from its most recent reconstruction (11th century).

The abbey was closed during the Revolution and the school became a saltpetre factory. Today, all that remains of the tremendous Benedictine holdings is the chapel and part of the monastery. Several pillars and arches in the structure belong to the 6th century building. All the rest is 11th century or thereafter. The frescoes were painted by Flandrin in the 19th century.

On exiting the church, turn right in rue Bonaparte, until you reach **L'Ecole des Beaux Arts** (The School for Fine Arts). This is a dignified and renowned institution which has been a source of aspiration and inspiration for art students worldwide and the breeding ground for many greats of the art world. Located at 17 Quai Malaquais since 1820, the building originally served as a monastery. The entrance is from 14 rue Bonaparte, but you can only visit when exhibitions are held in what was once the monastery church.

Following the bank of the Seine to the right you will come

a classical building with impressive pillars and a large dome. This is the **Institute de France**, established on the instructions of Cardinal Mazarin, in the late 17th century, as a school for higher learning for students from the remote areas in France. Napoleon changed the function of the institute in 1805, and it became the home of the different academies headed by the distinguished "French Academy", known as the "Immortal", rank among its 40 members leading personalities in France. Inside, you can see the Mazarin Library, which started out as the private collection of the cardinal, but which grew over the years. Today, it contains thousands of volumes, among them ancient and rare manuscripts. Open daily 10am-8pm. Closed Saturday and Sunday.

On leaving Institute Francais, turn right to reach **Hôtel des Monnaies** (Numismatic Museum) at 11 Quai Conti, 6^{e}, tel. 40.46.56.66. Open Tues.-Sun. 11am-5pm. Admission 10f. You can only visit the mint on Tues. and Fri. from 2:15pm. The opulent building on the Seine, completed in 1775 as the Royal Mint, presently houses exhibits of coins and minting tools. It also produces medallions and various coins which may be purchased there. Custom mintings on any theme and for any event may be specially ordered.

Return west along the bank of the Seine, Quai Voltaire, until you come across two museums, one new and in the news, the other older and more modest. We will start with the latter — **Musée de la Légion d'Honneur**, which is at 2 rue de Bellechasse, 7e, tel. 45.55.95.16, Solferino metro station. Open daily 2-5pm, closed Mon. Admission 10f, Sun. free. The museum is located in Hotel de Salm, an 18th century edifice occupied for a certain time by Napoléon Bonaparte. When the Emperor established the Legion of Honor in 1802, the palace became its headquarters. It was burned to the ground during the Paris Commune years, only to be rebuilt in 1878 exactly along the original lines. Today it houses the offices of the Chief Commander of the Legion, and this museum which commemorates the annals of the French order, its counterparts worldwide and the order of the medieval knights.

Exactly across the road from the Legion of Honor, is the gate to **Le Musée d'Orsay** at Place Henri de Montherlant, tel. 45.49.48.14. Solferino metro station. Open daily 10am-6pm, Thurs. until 9:45pm. Closed Monday. Take into account the long line at the entrance. Entrance 23f, Sunday 12f. The Gare d'Orsay railroad station building (const. 1900) has recently been converted into a museum. Many feel that today, from a number of aspects, this is one of the best museums in the world. While castles, palaces, monasteries and churches have often been used to house museums, a train station is quite a novelty. In the decision to establish the museum here, the great unusual structure of metal and glass, was protected from demolition. The central hall has been preserved in its original dimensions, 104 ft. (32 m) high, 131 ft. (40 m) wide and 452 ft. (138 m) long, as has the huge clock over the main entrance originally placed there for the convenience of the train commuters.

The museum, devoted to the second half of the 19th and the first years of the 20th century, exhibits collections of paintings, sculpture, decorative art, graphics, photography, cinema and architecture. Its construction cost the French taxpayer 1.08 billion francs.

On entering the museum, look up at the huge area of the domed roof, which is decorated in a pattern resembling squares of chocolate. The main avenue, on the entrance level, Rez-de-Chaussée which stretches across the length of the hall, is devoted to sculpture of the 1850-1870 period. Represented are works by Merciere d'Angers, Carpeaux, Pradier and others. From the avenue, the paths lead to the various halls, exhibiting paintings, architecture, furniture, decorative arts, etc.

In the halls on the right (A and C), are works by Michel Ingres, Delacroix, Chasseriau and historical portraits from the years 1850-1880. Worthy of special mention is Ingres' *The Spring*, which created a furor when it was first displayed in 1856. In the farther hall, you can see works by Gustave Moreau, De Chavannes and Degas, painted up to 1870. This provides an interesting look at works which were angrily rejected by the critics, and creations of many of the "lone" artists during the Second Empire.

On the left, in Halls B and D, there is an exceptional collection of works by truly great artists such as: Millet, Corot, Courbet, Manet, Monet, Renoir (until 1870), and others. Particularly impressive is the hall devoted to Gustave Courbet, which features, among other outstanding works, his famous painting of the *Studio*. Also of interest are the works by Honoré

Daumier, who ironically is remembered because of his caricatures which were originally banned. Perhaps the *pièce de résistance* here is Manet's *Luncheon on the Grass*.

The furthest sections, E and F, are devoted to architecture. Famous names here include Viollet le Duc, Morris and others. You can walk along a transparent floor and look, above and below, at a model depicting the area around the opera. Here you can also climb to the top two interior towers which lead onto small balconies which provide an incredible view of the entire museum area. After descending the tower, take the elevator to the floor above, *niveau supérieur*, on the left, which leads to exhibits devoted to the Impressionists and neo-Impressionists.

In the long and narrow Hall K, which is divided up into several smaller rooms, you can see an unparalleled collection of works by the greatest among the Impressionists: Monet, Renoir, Pissarro, Sisley, Van Gogh, Cézanne and others. (Many of these works were previously housed in the Jeu de Paume Museum). In a collection as outstanding as this, it is difficult to say which works deserve your special attention. Nevertheless, there are a few which cannot go unmentioned such as Monet's *Gare St. Lazare in Paris*, the *Windmill of La Gallette* by Renoir, Van Gogh's famous *Yellow Room* and Cézanne's *Card Players*.

Further along, in the spacious Halls L and M, you can see a selection of works by neo-Impressionists such as Seurat, Toulouse-Lautrec and Gauguin, including his painting *White Horse*.

On the same floor between the two sections, you can take a break at the museum coffee shop, which has the same opening hours as the museum. Near the coffee shop are the steps going down to the mezzanine level, *niveau médian*. Even if you are tired by now, this final floor of the museum should not be missed as it contains many wonderful and varied treasures.

In the left hand corner (Hall P), the exhibits are devoted to the decorative arts during the Third Republic, and sculpures by Rodin, Bourdelle, Maillol, Josef Berenner and others.

Further along, in Hall S, you can see "Salon" paintings from 1880-1900, examples of Naturalism and Symbolism, as well as works by foreign artists. In the various rooms in Hall U,

Musée d'Orsay — exterior and interior

there is a superb exhibiton of Art Nouveau. This form of decorative art emerged towards the beginning of this century, and is characterized by its rich ornamentation and sharp linearity.

In the right-hand corner of the mezzanine level is an exhibition on the beginning of photography and the cinema. It is interesting to see the birth of these art forms, which today plays so great a part in our lives. There are continuous screenings of the earliest movies.

Near this exhibition is the museum restaurant, which is an experience in itself. The colorful decor, with walls covered with pictures depicting mythological scenes, make eating here very special. Meals cost about 100-150f per person. Open from 11:30am, serves lunch and dinner. Closed on Sunday evening.

Before entering the museum you should keep the following in mind:
You must leave bags, carry-alls and umbrellas at the coat check.
You can take photographs, without a flash. No photographing of temporary exhibitons.
French speakers can enjoy a guided tour of the museum, daily at 11am, 1pm, and Thurs. on 7pm. Leaves from the reception desk.
A proper visit to Musée d'Orsay takes at least one full day.

Les Halles — Tomorrow's Paris Today

In the 1970s, the Les Halles Quartier was spoken of as "a place of tomorrow". Two large projects were in progress at the time: the **Pompidou Center for Art and Culture** and **Forum des Halles** — a giant underground commercial complex where the city's produce market once stood. These enterprises, now complete, have transformed the area between the eastern corner of Quartier 1, the western corner of Quartier 4, and the southwestern corner of Quartier 3.

To reach Les Halles, take the metro to the Châtelet or Les Halles station or bus lines 21, 29, 38, 47, 70, 81 or 85.

Forum des Halles occunies the site where Paris' great produce market once stood between the 12th century and 1969. The market was relocated to Rungis (near Orly) that year and four subterranean floors of shops were dug into the earth. Open at 1979, the complex at 1-7 rue Pierre Lescot is built around a circular plaza embellished by a statue of *Pygmalion* by Julio Silva. An innovative design was created using glass and aluminium as principal building materials.

The center has hundreds of shops which sell jewelry, fashion clothing, gifts, books, and everything else imaginable. There are also 12 restaurants, cinemas, 2 large parking lots and a small branch of **Musée Grévin** with, among other exhibits, a reconstruction of a late 19th-century Parisian street. Open daily 10:30am-6:45pm, Sunday 1-7:15pm, tel. 40.26.28.50. On the first floor there is also a **Holography Museum**, devoted to optical tricks, using laser beams and rays of light to create three-dimensional images. Open daily 10:30am-7pm, Sunday 1-7pm, tel. 42.96.96.83.

Behind the **Forum**, there is a large balcony which overlooks a unique garden, designed in mixed classical-modern style. There is a playground for children (there is a fee for use of the apparatus), a miniature train in turn-of-the-century style and an unusual "modern" sundial. When the sun shines, the rays are picked-up by an optical fibre which transmits them to the hour marks engraved in the stone. At the far end

LES HALLES, LE MARAIS, THE ISLANDS

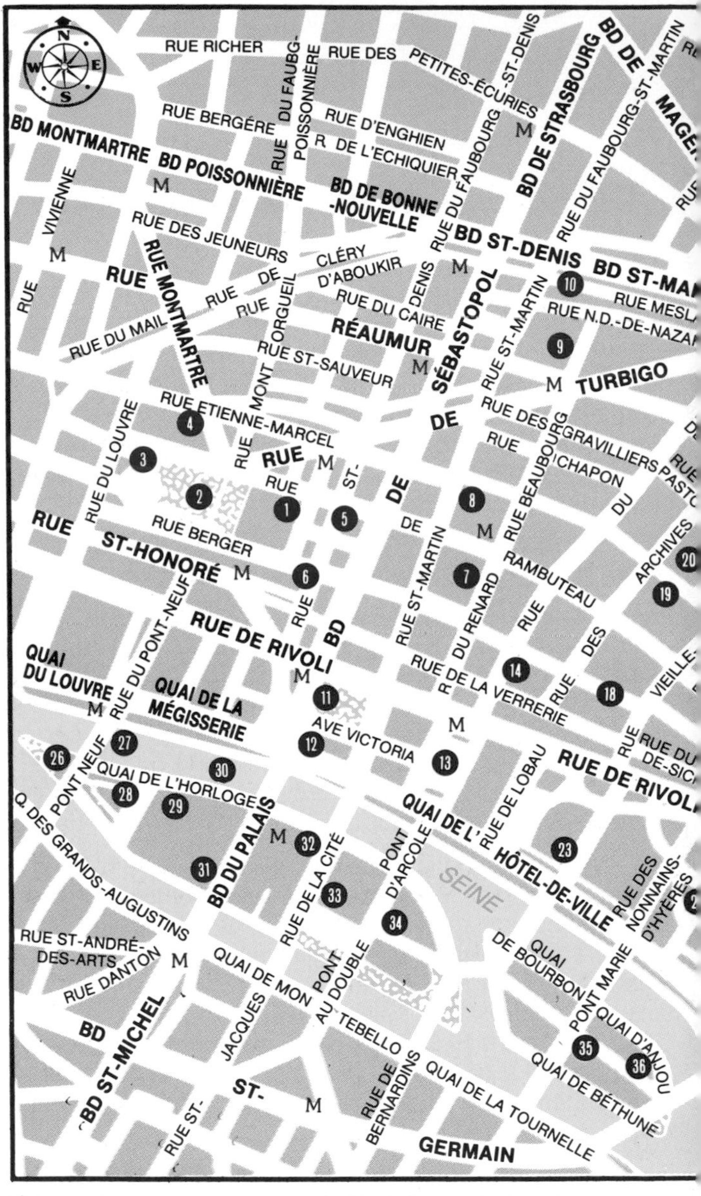

index

1. Forum des Halles
2. Garden of the Forum des Halles
3. Parc Océanique Cousteau
4. Saint Eustache Church
5. Rue Saint-Denis
6. Place des Innocents
7. Centre George Pompidou
8. Le Quartier de l'Horloge
9. St-Nicolas-des-Champs Church
10. Musée National des Techniques
11. Tour St.-Jacques
12. Place Châtelet
13. Hôtel de Ville
14. Bazar de l'Hôtel de Ville
15. Hôtel de Sully
16. Place des Vosges
17. Hôtel Carnavalet
18. Rue des Rosiers (Jewish Quarter)
19. Hôtel de Soubise

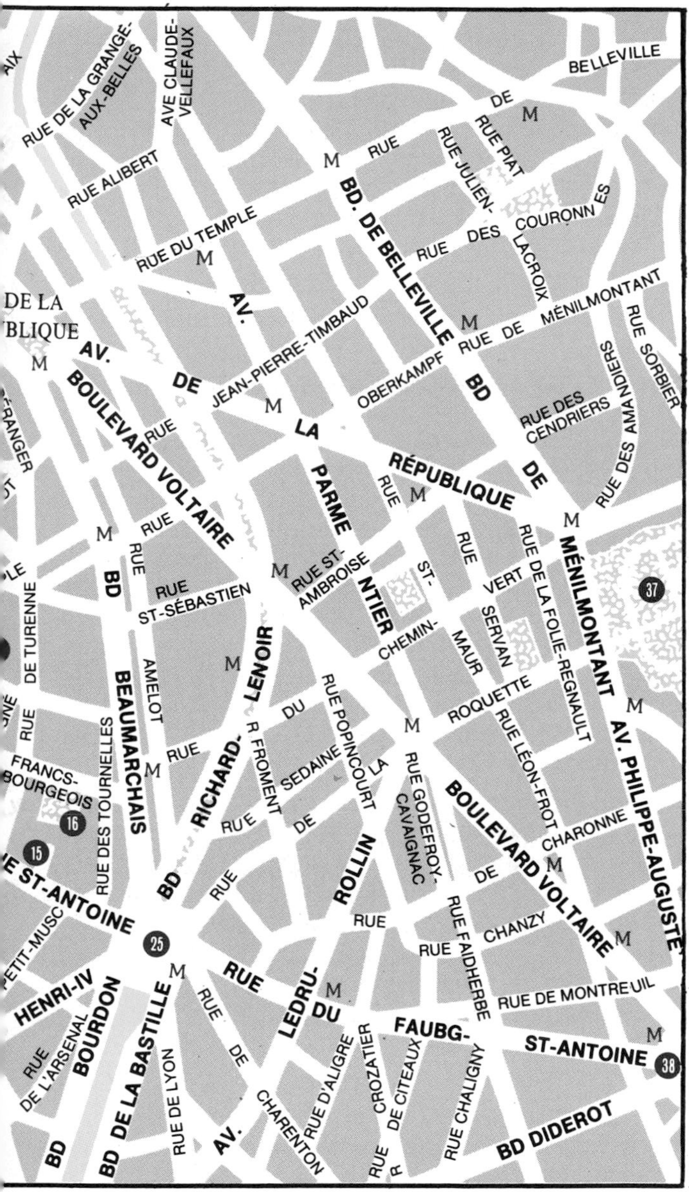

20. Hunting Museum
21. Musée Picasso
22. Hôtel Libéral-Bruand
23. Mémorial du Martyr Juif Inconnu
24. Hôtel de Sens
25. Place de la Bastille
26. Vert Galant
27. Pont Neuf
28. Place Dauphine
29. Palais de Justice
30. La Conciergerie
31. Sainte-Chapelle Church
32. Flower Market
33. Paris' Museum of Archeology
34. Cathédrale de Notre-Dame-de-Paris
35. Berthillon
36. Hôtel Lambert, Luzon Palace
37. Cimetière du Père Lachaise
38. Place de la Nation

of the garden, your attention is captured by the impressive round structure, built towards the end of the 19th century, and which today serves as the city's Trading Center. Next to it, facing the garden, stands a remnant of the palace built for Catherine de Medici, in the latter half of the 16th century. The "astrological pillar", topped by a metal structure was intended for use by her personal astrologer.

To the right stands the massive edifice of **Saint-Eustache Church**, built at the beginning of the 17th century in Gothic style. The building was financed by contributions from the merchants of the wholesale market. The church impresses one by its very size, some 330 ft. (100 m) long and more than 130 ft. (40 m) wide. Many well-known people began or ended their lives within the walls of this church. Cardinal Richelieu, the playwright Molière and Madame de Pompadour were all baptised here; The church is also where the funeral services of Mirabeau, La Fontaine, Colbert, and Mozart's mother (1778) were all held. The historical link to music of Saint-Eustache Church was affirmed when, in 1855, Berlioz conducted his recently composed *Te Deum* for the first time here. You will no doubt notice the colorful memorial stone erected to commemorate the Les Halles wholesale market which vacated the area in February 1969.

West of the church, at 6 rue Coquillère, is the very famous restaurant *Au Pied de Cochon* (Pig's Foot). The restaurant, which is open 24 hours daily, is always lively and bustling. You can enjoy good food in a gay Parisian atmosphere, with late 19th century decor enhancing the three floors of the establishment. The specialty of the house is, of course, pig's trotters, which are roasted and stuffed with goose liver. The restaurateurs report that they serve 80,000 portions of this dish annually to their patrons. A meal costs about 250f per person.

Near the church, on the eastern side of *Les Halles*, another very special attraction awaits you, **Parc Océanique Cousteau**. The brainchild of Jacques-Yves Cousteau, one of the greatest explorers of the oceans' depths, the park was set up in 1988. The ideology behind its establishment is best summed up by Cousteau himself: "People protect things they like. This park will give them the reasons to admire and better understand the underwater world which we are trying to preserve."

The park has reconstructed a small ocean, and visitors embark on an enchanted underwater journey in a small submarine, accompanied by recorded commentaries by Costeau. You can also travel into the stomach of a whale, and learn about the anatomy of this wonderful giant, which is 82 ft. (25 m) long and whose tongue is the size of an elephant! There is an exhibition devoted to the three states of water: liquid, gas and ice, and the role of water in the human body. The exhibition, of course, also surveys Costeau's adventures beneath the ocean, his work and discoveries.

West of the *Forum* is **rue Saint Denis** which has been converted into an effervescent pedestrian mall lined with cafés, shops, and fast-food restaurants, of which that belonging to the *Free Time* chain is recommended. As one heads north, the ambience of the street changes: the northern stretch is a crowded center of confection wholesalers... and prostitutes. The latter, taking up position day and night at house entrances and street corners, do not seem to bother the throngs of people on the street at all. Paris...

If you continue along the street in the direction of bd. St.-Denis, you will reach rue Blondel on the right. This small passageway was used for several scenes in the film *Irma La Douce*, about a kind-hearted prostitute. Her "pals" can be seen along the street waiting for customers, looking as if they just stepped out of the movie. Many tourists make do with just a quick peek!

Returning to Forum des Halles, go west to rue Berger which crosses bd. de Sebastopol. On the way look at the **Place des Innocents**, which until the end of the 18th century served as the burial grounds for over 2 million bodies. Their bones were exhumed and reinterred to the Catacombes, and the area was used as a vegetable market. The lovely fountain which graces the square was built in 1549, and was transferred here after the cemetery was relocated. *Café Costes*, today one of the more fashionable, and recommended cafés, stands in one corner of the square. It is worth taking advantage of the café's restrooms because of their exceptional design.

From here, walk about 400 m to 120 rue Saint-Martin where **Centre George-Pompidou** is located. The Center, also known as **Beaubourg**, the former name of the area, is open weekdays noon-10pm, Sat.-Sun. 10am-10pm; closed

Entrance to Forum des Halles

Place des Innocents

The Pompidou Center

Tues. Information on activities, tel. 42.77.11.12. Admission: Museum 20f, temporary exhibitions 16f, Sun. free.

The **Pompidou Center** made its 1977 debut amid cacophonous public controversy fueled by the epithets which the French language affords its speakers. Visitors will understand why. The architectural creation of Richard Rogers and Renzo Piano is a stunning tangle of utility pipes in shades of green, red and blue. All the conduits — ventilation, drainage, electricity — which are usually buried in the walls have been left in public view here. Even the escalators mount the building's five stories from the outside in order to leave more room inside. The escalators slide up and down in glass tubes, allowing visitors to take in the scenery. The top floor gazes onto the picturesque rooftops of Paris.

The interior has exhibition halls for modern art and contemporary industrial and environmental development; an institute for the study of musical acoustics (not open to the public); a large public library with over one million items: books, newspapers, records, slides, videos and microfilm (no user's fee); a children's library, a cinématheque, a theater, a concert hall and a self-service restaurant.

The plaza at the base of the Center is occupied almost every rainless day by magicians, singers, musicians, fire-eaters, actors, mimes and acrobats who perform for passers-by in return for coins which they collect in hats after performing.

North of the plaza (left when facing the Pompidou Center), is **Le Quartier de L'Horloge**, the Clock Quarter, comprised entirely of new tasteful houses built when the whole area was revamped. A covered passageway, **Passage de L'Horloge**, lined with shops, leads you to a small plaza. On the right hand side of the plaza, look up and see the clock which gave the area its name. Looming 13 ft. (4 m) high, and weighing 2,200 pounds (1000 kg), this unusual clock statue has a human form. Titled *The Protector of Time*, it portrays a man armed with a sword warding off a threatening threesome: a crab, a dragon and a bird — symbolizing sea, earth and sky. On every hour between 9am-10pm, he fights with one of the three creatures, facing the three of them at noon, 6pm and 10pm. This dramatic work was created between 1975 and 1979 by the artist Jacques Monstaire.

On the opposite side of the Pompidou Center, in the south, stands a plaza dedicated to the composer Igor Stravinsky, with a colorful and amusing fountain. Playing around in the fountain are statues by Jean Tingali and Niki de Saint-Paul.

This plaza is located near the **Saint-Merri Church**. Built in Gothic style, construction of the church was completed towards the end of 17th century. The pride of church is its huge antique organ, and recitals of religious music are often presented here.

Return to bd. Sebastopol, turn south, and walk 275 yards (250 m) to rue de Rivoli. There, in the middle of a public park, is **Tour (Tower) St.-Jacques**. Built in 1522, the tower which stands 170 ft. (52 m) high, was attached to a medieval church. The church itself was destroyed in 1797 by revolutionaries and only the tower was spared as it was used as a lead factory. The tower is no less famous as the site of Pascal's barometric experiments in 1648. Today, at the foot of the tower, there is a colorful carrousel which is lots of fun for children.

The south-eastern corner of the garden leads onto a plaza known as **Châtelet**. Gracing the plaza are two large and impressive halls, dating back to the second half of the 19th century, belonging to two old cultural institutions. The **Paris Musical Theater**, formerly the famous Opera House, now mainly stages ballet perfomances, and the **Municipal Theater**, as its name implies, is the venue for theatrical productions.

The impressive Paris City Hall, **Hôtel de Ville**, is 220 yards (200 m) farther east on rue Rivoli. Free guided tours are given every Monday at 10:30am, tel. 42.76.40.40.

Hôtel de Ville, dedicated in 1874, was built as a replica of the previous City Hall which burnt down in 1871. The plaza in front of the building was an execution ground until the Revolution. Some of France's most notorious criminals, including Ravaillac, La Voisin and Cartouche, were brought here to be burned, hanged or beheaded.

Hôtel de Ville resumed its function as the Mayor's headquarters in 1977 when all the *quartiers* of Paris were reunited into one municipal system. Jacques Chirac, elected Mayor that year, still holds the position, and today doubles as Prime Minister.

Near Hôtel de Ville, at 52 rue Rivoli, is another great Paris department store, *Bazar de l'Hôtel de Ville*. Known simply as B.H.V., this establishment specializes in, among many other items, housewares, hardware, and do-it-yourself materials

Additional points of interest
Le Musée National des Techniques, 270 rue Saint-Martin, tel. 42.71.24.14, Réaumur-Sébastopol metro station. Open daily 1-5:30pm, Sunday 10am-5:15pm, closed Monday. The museum (and the technical school found here) were established in the 18th century by the leaders of the revolution in an attempt to teach the people "serious" professions. As a first step, they also exhibited the mechanical toys which used to amuse the royal family, including a musical robot: *The Timpani Player*, built especially for Marie-Antoinette.

The museum also houses a collection of antique clocks of different types, varied and strange machines and exhibits from the early development of transport such as trains and cars, including a steam car. You can also view old cameras, optical machinery and many more such objects.

Nearby, at no. 254 rue Saint-Martin, stands **St.-Nicholas des**

At Place Stravinsky

Tour St-Jacques — The barometric experiment

Hôtel de Ville — City Hall

Place du Châtelet — Théâtre Musical

Champs Church. Construction on this edifice began in the 12th century, in Gothic style, but the majority of the work was carried out in the 15th century. The entrance hall, built in renaissance style, was added later on. Exhibited here are religious works by various artists from the 17th, 18th and 19th centuries. The antique organ was placed here at some point during the 18th century.

Le Marais — Yesterday's Nobility

Le Marais, in the eastern sections of *Quartiers* 3 and 4, is one of the most beautiful, interesting and ancient districts of Paris. Within it is the Jewish Quarter, le Quartier Juif. Take the metro to the Hôtel de Ville and St-Paul stations or the Bastille and Chemin-Vert stations, or bus 20, 29, 69, 76 or 96.

Paris' oldest homes are located in Le Marais, such as the house at 3 rue Volta which was built around 1300 and 51 rue Montmorency, erected in 1407.

Between the 15th and the 18th centuries, Le Marais was the favorite place for the Paris aristocracy to reside. During the 17th century, many noblemen graced the *quartier* with vast mansions, which included inner courts for coaches and horses and hidden gardens in the rear.

The eccentricities in the fashion of nobility tend to be quite unpredictable and in the 18th century, Le Marais suddenly went out of style and its noble residents migrated to St-Germain. The *quartier* lost its glitter when the new population was unable to maintain its level and a gradual state of deterioration and neglect has set in over the years.

The man who saved Le Marais, at perhaps the eleventh hour, was author Andre Malraux. As de Gaulle's Minister of Culture, he had Le Marais declared a protected area in the mid 1960s. As such, its homes were spared from any alteration, renovation or destruction which would harm their character. A large-scale reconstruction and clean-up project got underway at the same time which ultimately restored the district's charm and grandeur.

In the heart of the *quartier*, on rue Pavée, was the so-called **Le Quartier Juif** (Jewish Quarter) of Paris. A Jewish community existed here for hundreds of years, during various periods. Even today, rue des Rosiers and nearby streets boast a variety of kosher restaurants, kosher food shops and Hebrew bookstores.

To imbibe the special atmosphere and charm of Quartier Le

Hôtel de Sully — Courtyard

Marais, one should wander through its streets, stroll down its narrow alleys, peer into its courts and examine its every corner. The urge to explore is especially strong here. Our tour encompasses a number of interesting sites dispersed throughout the *quartier*.

If approaching from the south, from rue de St. Antoine, pass by Hôtel De Sully (you can go in to admire its two lovely interior courtyards), and turn north on rue de Birague. Continue to the end until you reach the charming quadrangle, **Place des Vosges**. The idea of building a plaza for festivities and outings at the site of a horse market was that of Henry IV. Though he gave it a name — La Place Royale — he did not live to see the work done as he was assassinated in 1610. The plaza was completed two years later.

The first celebration to be held here was the marriage of Louis XIII to Anne of Austria in April 1612. The royal nuptials were accompanied by 150 blasting trumpets and 1,000 mounted knights presenting arms. Commemorating the day, in the center of the garden, which takes up most of the plaza, stands of statue of the groom — Louis XIII.

The square-shaped array of houses on the square was occupied in various periods, for different durations, by some

Place des Vosges — Statue of Louis XIII

of the most famous figures in French history. No. 21 was the home of Cardinal Richelieu; No. 6, of author Victor Hugo and No. 8, of poet Théophile Gautier and author Alphonse Daudet.

Today, too, after a period of decline, the plaza is considered a fashionable and prestigious place to reside. Jacques Lang, Minister of Culture, has a flat overlooking the plaza. Art galleries, antique shops and restaurants operate under the arcades.

If you arrive at Place des Vosges at lunchtime, or you simply feel like relaxing over a light meal, there are two establishments which are worthy of notice here. *Eurydice*, at no. 20, serves light refreshment in a charming atmosphere with *trompe-l'oeil* decor. If you're not that hungry, you can enjoy a cup of tea with a sumptuous slice of cake — cheese, nut, chocolate, etc. — for which the restaurant is well-known. 27f per serving. Open from noon until 7pm, stays open later in summer.

For a more substantial meal, try *La Guirlande De Julie*, at no. 25, tel. 48.87.94.07. The restaurant is ornately decorated, in the opulant style of yesteryear. Traditional French cuisine. Particularly recommended is the *confit de cuisse de canard au cidre*. Open daily until 11pm, closed Monday and Tuesday.

Right next door to the restaurant, at no. 23, is an "antique" shop, which is very colorful and lots of fun because of the huge collection of serious "junk" which is on display.

Victor Hugo's home for 15 years, at 6 Place des Vosges, was declared **Musée Victor Hugo** in 1902. His furnishings, writing desk, various personal belongings and hundreds of his drawings, are on display. Open daily 10am-5:40pm, closed Mon. Admission 15f, Sun. free.

Some of the mansions of Le Marais are "musts" since they are treasures of architecture and charm which attest to a glorious past. If you don't have time to visit them, at least take a look from the outside.

L'Hôtel Carnavalet, 23 rue de Sévigné, 4e, tel. 42.72.21.13. Open daily 10am-5:40pm, closed Mon. Admission 15f, 7.50f with student card.

The building itself dates from the mid-16th century, and was expanded roughly a hundred years later. Marquise de Sévigné, a daughter of nobility who was a noted hostess and patron of contemporary philosophers, lived there in the late 17th century. Today the house serves as a museum chronicling the history of Paris and its inhabitants, from the early Renaissance period, through the reign of François I until the end of the 19th century. Its exhibit includes engravings, paintings, sculpture, furniture and *objets d'art*. Anyone interested in studying the past of Paris has to find time for a visit to this museum. One wing is devoted to the Revolution years. Its display includes the infamous guillotine, the armchair where Voltaire died in 1778 and more. One may also visit Marquise de Sévigné's magnificent rooms.

Exiting the museum to the right stretches rue Des Franc Bourgeois, and whoever is still under the influence of all the lovely *objets d'art* from the musuem, can take home something beautiful from no.13. This unusual store, *L'Arlequin*, stocks glass items from different periods, suited to nearly everyone's pocket. Open 12-7pm. Closed Sunday and Monday and a few weeks each summer. Take care not to break anything!

L'Hôtel Guénégaud, 60 rue des Archives, 3e, tel. 42.72.86.43. Open weekdays. 9:30am-6pm, closed Tues. Admission 10f. The building, erected in 1651, is noted for its lovely Classical court. It presently houses **Musée de la Chasse** with its comprehensive collection of weapons, stuffed animals and *objets d'art* associated with hunting, nature and the animal world.

Hôtel de Soubise, 60 rue de Francs-Bourgeois, 3e, tel. 42.77.11.30. Open daily 2-5pm, closed Tues. Admission 4f, Sun. 2f.

The house, owned by the famous Guise family in the 16th and 17th centuries, was subsequently appropriated from those noblemen by the Prince of Soubise. He expanded it and embellished it with the works of some of the best-known artists of his time: Van Loo, Lemoyne and Boucher.

Today the building, and a number of adjoining buildings, house **Les Archives Nationales: Musée de l'Histoire de France**. Some extraordinary historical documents are exhibited here, such as the wills of Louis XIV and Napoleon; letters by Voltaire and a one-of-a-kind portrait of Joan of Arc by an anonymous contemporary painter. The private rooms of the Prince and Princess of Soubise are also interesting and impressive.

In 1927, Musée des Archives Nationales spilled into the building next door, **Hôtel de Rohan**. There its documents take up 175 miles (280 km) of shelves!

Hôtel Salé, 5 rue de Thorigny, 3e, tel. 42.71.25.21. Open daily 10:00am-5:15pm, Wed. till 10pm, closed Tues. Admission 20f. One of the loveliest buildings in Le Marais from the nobility period, it was erected in 1656 as the residence of De Fontenay, the concessionaire (collector) of the royal tax on salt.

The building was extensively renovated in 1985 and refurbished as **Musée Picasso**. The Government of France acquired much of the artist's personal collection in lieu of the inheritance tax his heirs would have had to pay. Picasso was one of the few artists of such stature who kept many of his own works. The museum exhibits 203 of his paintings, 158 sculptures, 16 collages, 29 engravings, 88 ceramic works and more than 3000 preliminary sketches, drawings and Picasso's *The Barefoot Girl*, which he painted at the age of 14. The exhibit also includes artwork which, though produced by other famous artists (including Renoir, Cézanne, Matisse, Braque and Miró), belonged to Picasso.

Here Picasso-lovers are given their first opportunity for a glimpse into his personal world, contemplate works which were never displayed prior to his death, and observe the various periods and stages of his work. The works are, in fact, displayed on the different levels, according to his different periods. In the basement you can view Picasso's more modern works, from the last years of the artist. The lobby level houses those works from the 1930s, across from which is the cafeteria overlooking the statue garden.

Works from Picasso's "Blue Period" are on the first floor, as are those done doing his "Rose Period" and his cubist and surrealistic paintings. Picasso's private collection can be seen on the second floor.

Additional points of interest

Hôtel Libéral-Bruand, 1 rue de la Perle, tel. 42.77.79.62. Open Tues.-Sat. 10am-noon, 2-5pm; closed in August. Admission 5f. During the 17th century this was the home of the famous French architect Libéral-Bruand, designer of Palais des Invalides and other notable structures. Today it houses **Musée Bricard** and an extensive collection of locks (doors, closets, safes, handles) and smithing tools used over the past two thousand years.

Hôtel de Sens, on the corner of rue de L'Hôtel de Ville and rue du Figuier, is one of the oldest palaces found in the *quartier*. It was built in mixed Gothic-Renaissance style, from 1475-1519, as the home of the Archbishop of Sens, Tristan de Salazare, as Paris was then under his realm of authority.

In 1606, Henry IV housed his ex-wife, Queen Margot de Valois, in this palace, and towards the end of the 17th century, it came into the possession of the nobleman, Philippe de Daro. Thereafter, the palace's history was less illustrious, and following the revolution it was divided up into apartments. The activity which took place within its walls was not suited to its exterior beauty which gradually began to fade. In 1911, however, it was purchased by the municipality of Paris, and underwent extensive renovations which were periodically halted until they were finally completed in 1961. In that year it became home to the **Fornay Library**, which specializes in fine and decorative arts.

Hôtel de Sens — The French Garden

Worthy of particular mention and of a special look is the garden behind the palace. The landscaping took from 1955-1957, and was done in the French gardening style typical of the end of the 16th century, with sculpted trees and flowerbeds laid out in geometric designs. Delightful!

Exiting Hôtel de Sens, turn right into rue Hôtel de Ville, and right again into rue Geoffroy-Lasnier until you come to the monument in honor of the Jewish Martyrs — **Mémorial du Martyr Juif Inconnu**. There is a small museum here to commemorate the victims of the holocaust, and archives housing various documents. Open 10am-12pm and 2-5pm, closed Saturday.

Not far from where we started this tour, next to Place des Vosges, is another plaza, famous because of its history — **Place de la Bastille**. This is, of course, a milestone in the history of France (and the world), because of events which took place here on 14th July 1789. At that time, there was a strong fortress, protected by eight towers, which was built in the second half of the 14th century, during the reign of Charles V, as part of Paris' defense system. Later, it was converted into a famous prison, for prisoners whom the King's court felt needed "special" guarding. Stories about what went on in the prison cells spread throughout Paris, among them that of the "Man in the Iron Mask" whose face no-one ever saw (and who is the subject of a number of films about that period). A very famous "tenant" of the prison was the Marquis de Sade, from whose name, because of the nature of his activities, the word sadism was derived.

The significance of the fortress explains why the revolutionaries chose to storm the Bastille and to rescue the seven prisoners inside its walls on that day, and why over the next few months they demolished it until there remained only a pile of rubble. The site became a popular spot for festivites. The memorial pillar, which today stands in the middle of the broad plaza actually commemorates the victims of the 1830 riots. Today, the plaza has been granted another opportunity to regain its popularity, due to the new opera house which is being built here — **L'Opéra de La Bastille**. The "old" Paris opera house, built over a century ago, is too small to cope with popular demand. In the last few years in France, there has been a great reawakening in this art form. In addition to which, the Socialist cabinets, which now dominate French government, wanted another opera house which would be accessible to the general population, who could come and enjoy first-rate opera.

The modern building, which has been designed by the architect Carlos Otto, resembles an office block. It comprises two auditoriums, studios for sets and costumes, offices and rehearsal space. The "large" auditorium can seat 2700 (in black velvet chairs), while the "small" hall has 1300 seats. The planners are hoping that it will be able to serve as the venue for hundreds of productions annually, large-scale and small, throughout the day and night. There will also be a public center for opera lovers, which will offer them the facilities of a large opera library with books, records, videos and an area for exhibitions.

The Islands: "Floating" on the Seine

Stand on **Pont des Arts** and look east, toward the prow-like tip of **Ile de la Cité**. This is the cradle of Paris, where, in the 3rd century BC, the Celtic Parisii tribe settled. Ile de la Cité and its "little brother", Ile St. Louis, are surrounded on all sides by the Seine and are packed with interesting sites, lovely spots and impressive historic and architectural monuments.

The metro reaches one end of the area at the Cité or Pont Neuf station and the other end at Pont Marie. By bus, take line 21, 47, 58, 70, 86, 87 or 96.

Pont Neuf (New Bridge), slicing across the western end of Ile de la Cité, is actually the oldest bridge in Paris. Henry III laid its cornerstone in 1578, and the work was completed in 1605, after a lengthy interruption. Henry IV was the first to cross it — on horseback, with his cohort of knights in tow. Its 12 arches are embellished with sculptured heads, humorously depicting a number of Henry IV's court. In the center of the bridge stands a statue of the King — a replica produced in 1818, after the original was melted down during the Revolution.

Stairs behind the statue lead to **Vert Galant**, a well-tended garden at the tip of the island (and at its original elevation). A narrow passageway leads from the other side of the bridge to **Place Dauphine**, a charming place built in the 17th century and named for the crown prince (Fr. *dauphine*) who later became Louis XIII.

One of those graceful Paris bistros whose universal reputations fuel the city's glory is *Caveau du Palais* (*caveau* meaning cellar), 19 Place Dauphine. Sip wines of exceptional quality and enjoy a selection of superb fish and meat dishes smoke-grilled over wood, while sitting amid the *Caveau's* ancient stone walls and under its wooden ceiling supports. Dessert lovers will not want to miss a glorious creation named *la marquise fondante au chocolat*. Price: approx. 300f per person. Service until 10:30pm, closed Sat. and Sun. tel. 43.26.04.28.

A bloc of impressive buildings rises east of the square. The

Palais de Justice

first is **Palais de Justice**. Enter from bd. du Palais. The side facing Place Dauphine is also rather impressive. Two stone lions stand guard on the stairway, 6 statues grace the façade while 2 Napoleonic eagles span their wings on the roof. Open Mon.-Fri. 9am-7pm; closed from mid-July until mid-September.

During the time of Roman rule, this was the original site of the palace of the Imperial Prefect. Subsequent French kings, made it their home, until Charles V, in the 14th century, used it as the site of his parliament while setting up his own residence in Palais de Louvre. The present name dates from the Revolution.

The plaza in front of the main entrance, *Cour de Mai*, gives one a view of the structure's impressive façade, renovated at the end of the 18th century. Inside are vast halls which housed the king and his noblemen in days of yore as well as members of Parliament in later years. During the Revolution, it was the seat of the notorious Revolutionary Court, from

Des bouquinistes — bookstalls on the river bank

which convicted prisoners were sent to the guillotine. The halls, damaged twice by fire over the years and renovated in their present form in 1870, are used today by the courts of Paris. Trials are usually public and tourists are welcome.

Next to Palais de Justice, somewhat tucked away behind its walls, is one of Paris' most beautiful churches: **Sainte-Chapelle**, 4 bd. du Palais; tel. 43.54.30.09. Usually open daily, 10am-5pm. The entrance is through an opening to the right of the large gate. Cross the courtyard to the left, and then turn right. This jewel of Gothic art, built by St. Louis in the mid-13th century, was used by the royal entourage when the rulers of France resided on the island. St. Louis wished to use this church as a repository for the "souvenirs" he had acquired from Emperor Beaudoin II of Byzantium: a remnant of the crown of thorns which Jesus wore during his crucifixion and part of the True Cross. (The authenticity of these artifacts has attracted different opinions; in any case, today they are kept in the Cathedral of Notre-Dame.)

The ground floor of the Sainte-Chapelle served court personnel, and the second floor was for the royal family. A surprising and magnificent burst of light descends through the lovely stained glass windows, which depict scenes from the New Testament, such as the life of Jesus and the vision of the Apocalypse.

During the Revolution, the rebels used Sainte-Chapelle for the storage of flour. During the Great Fire of 1871 it was saved from destruction.

The third site in the chain of massive buildings known today as Palais de Justice is the **Conciergerie**. Enter through a small gate north of the building. This structure often served as a prison where some of the greatest criminals in French history were incarcerated. During the Revolution, thousands of convicts were sent from its gloomy cells and torture chambers to the guillotine. The Conciergerie is open daily, 10am-6pm (4:25pm in winter). The tour only includes certain parts of the building. It begins in a large impressive hall, la Salle des Gens d'Armes, built in Gothic style. This is probably the largest medieval hall of its type in Europe stretching 230 ft (70 m) long and 88ft (27 m) wide, with a ceiling held up by dozens of arches. At the end of the hall, to the left, steps lead to what used to be the palace kitchen in the 16th century. Judging from its size and from the four ovens, one can just imagine the quantities of food prepared for the courtiers upstairs!

Opposite the Palais de Justice, across the boulevard to the right, in another monumental edifice, is one of the headquarters of the **Paris Police**. Rue de Lutèce, which runs below it, was turned into a wide pedestrian mall in 1989. Next to it is a flower market (open daily 8am-7:30pm, closed Mon.), which is also the site of a picturesque bird market held every Sunday, when the sound of thousands of birds twittering in little cages fills the air. Farther on is **Hôtel-Dieu**, a large hospital founded in the 17th century. Even for those bursting with good health, it's worthwhile taking a peek into the very impressive interior courtyard of the hospital, from the main entrance facing south.

At the southeast corner of the island stands the **Cathédrale de Notre-Dame-de-Paris** and its two towers, 230 ft (69 m) in height. Notre-Dame has become an emblem of Paris over the years. Poets, authors and artists lend it prominence in their works. One example is Victor Hugo's novel *The Hunchback of Notre Dame.* Quasimodo, sounder of the cathedral bells, resides at the highest echelon of world literature.

Its centrality is such that Notre-Dame is customarily used as point zero in measuring every distance from Paris to other cities in France or Europe.

In 1163, Father Maurice de Soli decided to erect a church where a temple to Jupiter had stood during the Roman conquest. Construction lasted many years and proceeded slowly, with long interruptions, and was finally completed only in 1330. The cathedral was damaged during the Revolution, its statues were shattered, treasures plundered and large bronze bells melted down. The building was expropriated by the revolutionary regime and was redesignated "The Hall of Wisdom".

In the 19th century, architect Viollet-le-Duc assumed the tremendous task of renovation. The architect did not settle for mere reconstruction but added his own contribution to the cathedral such as the pointed bronze tower which soars skyward from the cathedral roof. During the great havoc of the Paris Commune in 1871, Notre-Dame was again pillaged. Put to the torch this time, it remained standing only because its walls were so solid.

Study the façade at the entrance which features a series of 28 stone replicas of kings of France, known as the Gallery of Kings. The three arches over the entrance doors depict scenes from the Christian canon and the lives of the cathedral's saints.

Inside, look up and follow the columns which climb interminably to the ceiling, 115 ft (35 m) high, a structure which dwarfs everything below. The internal area of the cathedral is approximately 6,500 sq. yards (5,500 sq.m), and can house some 10,000 people. In the middle of the inner hall, to the right and the left of the apse, are the great stained glass windows which on sunny days admit beams of light. Around the hall and along the walls are the chapels. Note their religious statues and paintings, most dating from the 17th century, and the confessional booths. Several Archbishops of Paris during the past few centuries are buried in the large eastern chapel.

The doorway to the treasures of Notre-Dame appears in the middle of the southern wall of the cavernous hall. Open daily, 10am-6pm, Sunday 2-6pm. Admission 15f. On display here are fragments of the True Cross (encased in a grand structure made of precious metals) and the remnants of the crown of thorns which, according to Christian tradition, Jesus wore to his death. Tapestries belonging to Marie Antoinette are on display as well.

On the river banks — home port

Outside the cathedral, at the northwestern corner, is an entrance to the 387-step (!) ascent to the church towers which affords a magnificent view of the city. Open daily, 10am-5:30pm (4:30pm in winter). Admission charged.

Beneath the square in front of Notre-Dame is **Crypte Archéologique**, Paris' Museum of Archeology, opened in 1980. To reach it, follow the steps at the northern edge of the plaza. Open daily, 10am-6pm (5pm in winter). Among the museum exhibits are the findings of new archeological digs from the Gallo-Roman period, cellars of medieval houses and a model depicting the historical development of Paris. Behind Notre-Dame and past a garden which stretches as far as the Seine, Pont St. Louis bears traffic to **Ile St. Louis** (previously known as Ile Notre-Dame). It was from here that King Louis the saint set out in 1267 on his last Crusade. His legacy is this island which bears his name.

During the 17th century, the island became a favored location for the residences of the noble and wealthy of France. Quite a few leaders, artists, writers and poets (of means, of course) made their homes here in subsequent centuries.

Many shops on the main street of the island, rue St. Louis en l'Ile, preserve the area's original flavor. No. 31, for example, is *Berthillon*, which makes and sells the most famous ice cream in Paris, in 27 flavors. It is difficult to know when the establishment is open since its owner often takes unexpected vacations. But, except for Monday and Tuesday, with a little luck and patience (there's usually a line), the gastronomical experience is worth waiting for.

There are a few other worthwile stops along this charming street. At no. 90 there is a lovely tea-salon, *Au Lys D'Argent*, which also serves light repast. *L'Epicerie* stands at no. 51. In this wonderful shop you can find a huge array of teas and jams, all in beautiful packaging. A real treat. No. 12 houses a Polish library on the ground floor. Raise your eyes to find a plaque commemorating the well-know engineer Philippe Lavon who, in 1799, discovered the priciple behind lighting and heating by means of gas. This used to be his home.

On the eastern side of the street, at no. 2, the palace **Hôtel Lambert** is located. It was built in 1640 by the royal architect to Louis XI, for the son of a very wealthy nobleman, Lambert de Torini. Many years later, there are still very famous tenants in this palace — Baron Rothschild and the actress Michèle Morgan.

A left turn at the end of the street, will bring you to the banks of the river, Quai D'Anjou on which stand the glorious homes of Paris' nobility during the golden age of the island in the 17th century. Some of the illustrious residents, whose windows overlooked the river are worthy of mention. No.9 was the home of the caricaturist and artist Honoré Daumier, while at Luzon Palace at no.17, lived, among others, the poet Baudelaire, the author Reiner Maria Rilke and the composer Richard Wagner. On the ground floor of no.19 lived, from 1899-1913, the sculptress Camille Claudel, lover of Auguste Rodin. In 1989 she underwent a "resurrection" when Isabelle Adjani portrayed the sculptress in a successful movie. From here, Camille was taken to a home for the insane, where she died in 1943.

Take a walk around the island on the riverbank sidewalk, and you can stop at **Musée Adam Mickiewicz**, 4-6 Quai d'Orléans, which commemorates the great Polish author and poet, 1798-1855, who lived here in the last years of his life. The modest museum also reserves space for the works of other Polish artists, including a special hall for Chopin. Open Thur., 3-6pm; closed during the summer. Admission free.

A Latin Quarter with Latin Charm

Le Quartier Latin occupies *Quartier 5* and something of *Quartier 6*, in the area customarily known as La Rive Gauche ("the Left Bank"). It was a great scholastic center as early as the Middle Ages and became a lodestone for the knowledge-thirsty throughout France and Europe. The language used in literary circles at the time, Latin, lends the *quartier* its name. It retains its scholarly imprint today too, though to a lesser extent than in the past; the Sorbonne (which is now only one part of Paris University), Collège de France and the College School of Administration are but a few of the academies situated here.

The *quartier's* young, transient population gives it a special atmosphere. During the 1968 "student revolution" the *Quartier* was a major battlefield between students and police. Cobblestones were ripped up for projectiles; fences and columns were uprooted for barricades and shops in the area were pillaged. In the end order was restored, accompanied with certain reforms and, a little later, the resignation of President de Gaulle — the bane of the students and the proletariate. No indication of the strife of that era remains today.

The earlier changes of Baron Haussmann's have survived to this day. Haussmann, the energetic builder (or destroyer, as some have claimed) of Paris, cleared away buildings and pushed through the *Quartier*'s two great boulevards, St. Michel and St.-Germain. A few streets — mainly east of bd. St.-Michel, ,near the Seine — were left untouched. Characteristics remaining from earlier times may be observed: overcrowding, buildings jammed together on both sides of the street, with predominantly 18th century style architecture.

This part of the *Quartier* is now a large Pedestrian Mall. Alongside it in either direction is the largest concentration of Greek restaurants in Paris, along with a wealth of bookstores, cinemas (clubs for art films and "good films"), cafes with a shoulder-to-shoulder youth clientele, and discotheques.

Almost everything takes place in a young, Bohemian atmosphere.

By metro, get off at Cardinal Lemoine, Luxembourg, St.-Michel or Maubert Mutualité. By bus, lines 21, 27, 38, 47, 63 or 96.

One way to explore the *Quartier* is in historical sequence. Start with **Musée des Thermes et de l'Hôtel de Cluny**, an interesting establishment at the corner of Bds. St.-Michel and St.-Germain, with a collection of medieval exhibits alongside the ruins of a Roman bath. Enter from behind at 6 Place Paul Painlevé, 5e, tel. 43.25.62.00. St.-Michel metro station. Open daily 9:45am-12:30pm, 2-5:15pm; closed Tues. Admission charged.

Stop in the court at the museum entrance and glance at the lovely facade of the building which was erected in the 15th century for monks of the Cluny Order. The well (notice the pulley lift) to the right of the entrance, still yields its abundant waters. Wandering between the rooms and the labyrinthine passages of the ancient monastery is an experience in itself.

Inside, enjoy the extensive collection of medieval sculpture, carvings and woven articles, along with more mundane artifacts such as keys, locks, fireplace tools, fences, weapons, money, jewelry, weights and containers of various kinds. One especially noteworthy feature here is the collection of tapestries. Its centerpiece, *The Lady and the Unicorn*, on display in a special hall on the second floor, is one of the most famous examples of this art form. The story of the matron and the unicorn are portrayed in six tapestries. It is known that the tapestry was commissioned by a wealthy merchant family from Lyons, but those who carried out the task remain anonymous.

Another source of surprise in this museum is the Hall of the Kings' Heads. In an unexpected archeological find, twenty-one sculpted heads, most damaged, were discovered in 1977 in a demolished cellar of an old office building on the Right Bank. They proved to belong to statues from the Gallery of Kings in the facade of the Cathedral of Notre-Dame. Torn down during the Revolution, they had been considered lost.

Enter another world by going on a tour of the remains of the 3rd century Roman bath house. Water for the baths was

THE LATIN QUARTER

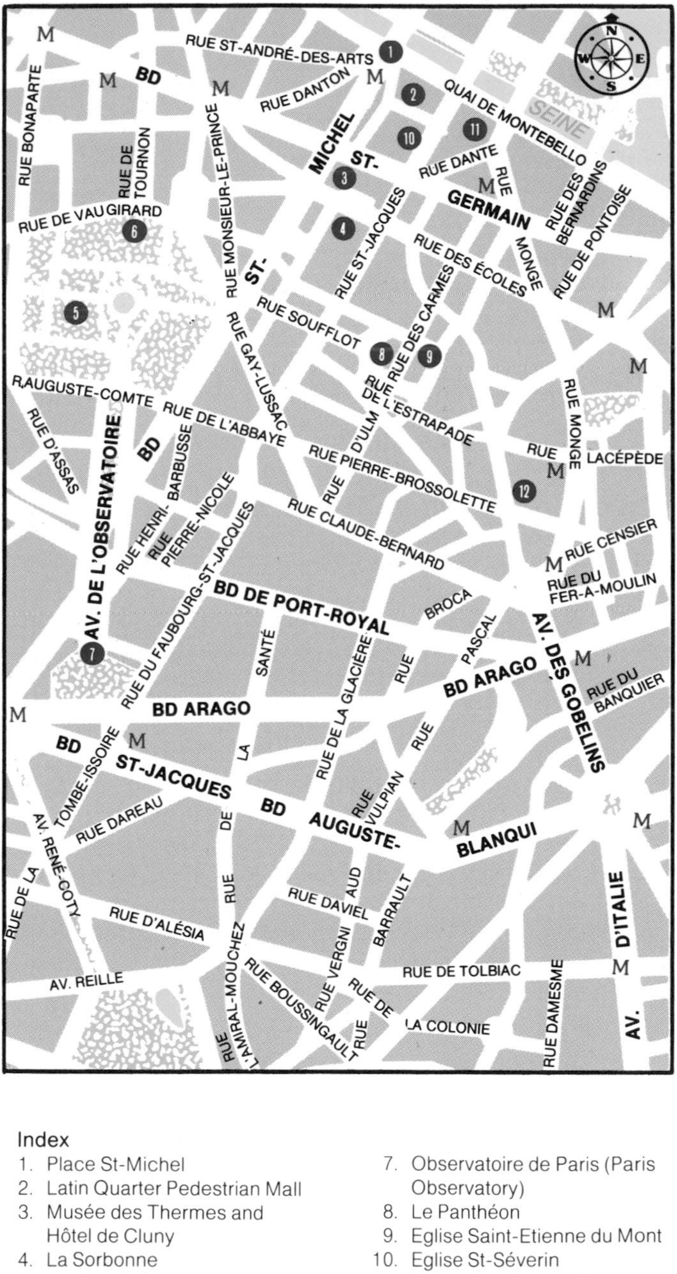

Index

1. Place St-Michel
2. Latin Quarter Pedestrian Mall
3. Musée des Thermes and Hôtel de Cluny
4. La Sorbonne
5. Jardins du Luxembourg
6. Palais du Luxembourg (French Senate)
7. Observatoire de Paris (Paris Observatory)
8. Le Panthéon
9. Eglise Saint-Etienne du Mont
10. Eglise St-Séverin
11. Eglise St-Julien-le-Pauvre
12. Rue Mouffetard

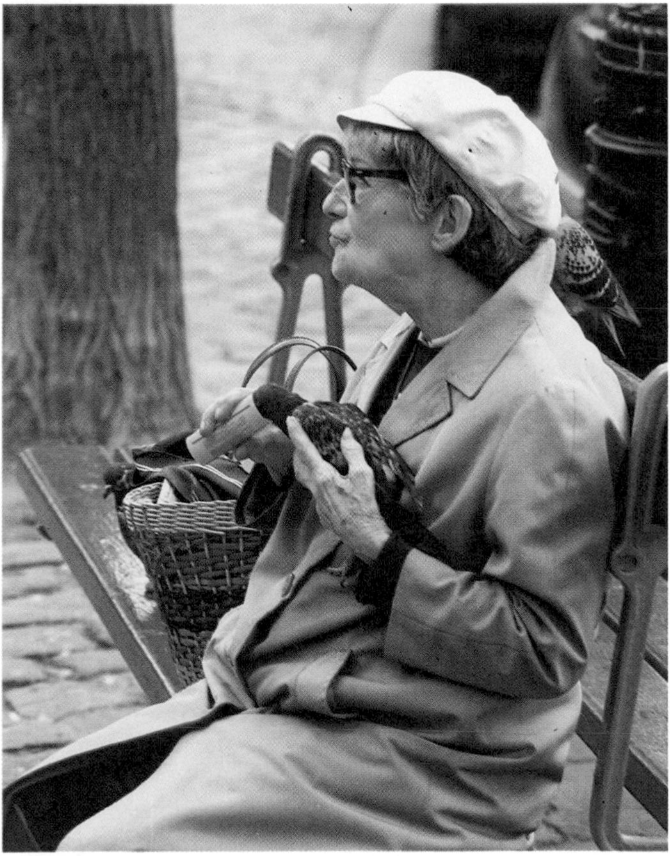

On the Place St.-Michel

brought from over 6 miles (10 km) away by means of an aqueduct.

The breathtakingly massive block of buildings across the square from Musée de Cluny is **La Sorbonne**. Crossing the yard of this university (embellished with an impressive sundial) and roaming its corridors, gives one a sense of history. The world-famous academy was founded in 1253 when Father Robert de Sorbonne, a nobleman and St. Louis' confessional priest, began to teach 16 students of theology in what very quickly became the key cultural and scientific institution in France and Europe. In the 22 study halls, built like small amphitheaters, generations of students have acquired knowledge.

The Sorbonne was renovated and expanded in the 17th century by Cardinal Richelieu. He is buried in the church which he added on to the institution.

Apart from a short and sad hiatus during the Revolution, the Sorbonne has never closed. Today it houses the College of the Humanities of l'Université de Paris. The Sorbonne is also famous for its large Baroque-style library building where more than 1,500,000 volumes are kept.

From the Sorbonne, return to bd. St.-Michel, turn left, and follow the avenue to **Place Edmond Rostand** (named for the Marseilles-born dramatist who created *Cyrano de Bergerac*, among other works). It is no coincidence that this street bears his name, because from the plaza, rue De Medici leads to the **Théâtre de l'Odéon**, which was established towards the close of the 18th century. Today, it is one of Paris' national theaters. To the right is **Jardin du Luxembourg**. The garden is open every day around the clock, but the palace, where the French Senate meets, may be visited only in organized groups. For details call tel. 42.34.20.60.

The palace, completed in 1624, was built for Marie de Médici, Henry IV's widow. She had purchased the land from the Duke of Luxembourg, and had architect Salomon de Brosse design a palace in the style of the Pitti Palace which had been her home in Florence. Marie dei Medici had planned to spend the rest of her life there but fate had other things in store. In 1630, after less than five years in the palace, she was exiled by the new king to Cologne. During the Revolution the palace was expropriated and used as a prison for two years. Its tenure as home of the Senate came later. The monastery next to it was demolished, and a charming garden was built where it had stood.

The structure to the west is known as **Petit Luxembourg**; and once served as the residence of the Duke. Today it is the home of the President of the French Senate.

The famous **Médici Fountain** is located in the palace park. Children float little sailboats in the round pool in the center of the garden. The garden's embellishments include statues of authors and poets including the likenesses of George Sand,

Paul Verlaine, Stendhal and Flaubert.

While strolling south on the avenue leading from the park (Jardins de L'Observatoire), notice the unusual fountain by sculptor Carpeaux. It incorporates the statues of four women, representing four continents, carrying a globe of bronze. The avenue finally leads you to the Paris observatory, **L'Observatoire de Paris**, construction of which commenced in 1667, making it one of the oldest such institutions in Europe. Today, it houses the International Ministry of Time, responsible for worldwide accuracy regarding "time", and **Musée de l'Observatoire de Paris**. The museum is only open on the first Saturday of each month, when there are guided tours. The lines are usually long, but those who are determined will be rewarded with seeing a collection of astrological measuring tools and other implements used for examing the heavenly bodies. Only recommended for those with a particular interest in astronomy.

We return northwards, and opposite the eastern exit of Jardin de Luxembourg, up rue Soufflot (named for the architect of the Panthéon), the highly impressive dome of **Le Panthéon** comes into view.

The Panthéon is open daily, 10am-12pm and 2-5pm. Only escorted groups, which depart every fifteen minutes, may visit the cellar, where the ashes of France's luminaries are kept. They include post-Revolution greats such as Mirabeau, Emile Zola, Voltaire, Jean-Jacques Rousseau, Victor Hugo, and Jean Jaurès (hero of the struggle against the Nazis). There is an entrance fee.

The Panthéon began as a church, after Louis XV vowed during a severe illness that, if he recovered, he would build a new church in place of the old Eglise de St. Geneviève which occupied the site. He kept his word, and building commenced in 1764. The revolutionaries decided to establish the place for the ashes of the nation's great. This was done, but the church prevented it for a while — until the death of Victor Hugo who was buried there, according to the decision of the leaders of the Third Republic to return the Panthéon, once and for all, to his eternal role.

The exterior of the building is certainly worth close examination, as it is considered by many to be the most impressive example of neo-classical architecture in Paris.

Inside, notice the collection of 19th-century paintings.

Next to the north-eastern corner of the Panthéon is the **Church of Saint-Etienne-du-Mont**, constructed in Gothic-Renaissance style at the close of the 15th century. The 16th century stained glass windows are worth a visit and the special design of the church gallery is also impressive.

Additional points of interest

In the crowded, pedestrian mall section of the Latin Quarter, east of bd. St.-Michel on rue des Prêtres St.-Séverin, is **L'Eglise St.-Séverin**. It is one of the best-preserved churches from the Middle Ages. Visit weekdays 11am-1pm, 3:30-7:30pm; Sun. 9am-1pm, 1:30-7:45pm. Closed Monday. Church music concerts, among others, are held here; consult bulletins posted inside for details.

Though not a large structure, St.-Séverin is noted for its beauty and harmony. Its windows are magnificent, as is its 15th-century bell (which once served as a fire alarm).

At the northern tip of the Latin *Quartier*, along the river opposite Notre-Dame, is **L'Eglise St.-Julien-le-Pauvre** on the street of the same name. The church, surrounded by gardens, is believed to be the oldest in Paris (construction began in 1170). Today it belongs to the Catholic Orthodox Church and mass is conducted in Latin. Open daily, 9am-1pm, 3-7pm.

Slightly behind l'Eglise St.-Julien-le-Pauvre, at 37 rue de la Bucherie (no phone) is one of the most cluttered bookstores in Paris — **Shakespeare and Company**. Enjoy its wide selection of bargains, while taking in the ongoing, spontaneous literary salon which bustles most hours of the day. Open noon-midnight.

On the other side of the church, toward the southwest, at 9 rue Lagrange is one of the 11 restaurants in the *Hippopotamus* chain, tel. 43.54.13.99. It serves a generous fixed-price menu of deliciously-dressed fresh salads and reasonable quality steaks grilled over coals and served with chips (French fries) and wine. The decor is functional and comfortable, and the restaurant is air-conditioned. Prices: approx. 70f for fixed-menu. Open daily until 1am.

At this stage, a stroll down rue Mouffetard is recommended.

Follow rue Monge to No. 56, the National School of Photography and Cinema, turn right onto rue Rollin, and follow it to a charming square, **Place de la Contrescarpe**. From here, emerges rue Mouffetard, an authentic and unspoiled remnant of Old Paris. The narrow streets here are packed with quaint little shops, creating a bustling market. Restaurants and cafes add to the hearty atmosphere. To reach the area directly, take the metro to Place Monge, and follow rue Ortolan west until rue Mouffetard.

Montparnasse — From Apollo to Hemingway

Every book lover must have encountered the name Montparnasse and for good reason. It is a lodestone for many important 20th century authors, who lived, played, drank and wrote there, immortalizing one locale or another in their books.

Montparnasse has been a literary district from the beginning. Literature students in the Sorbonne gave the quarter its name somewhere in the 17th century, selecting Mount Parnasse where, in Greek mythology, Apollo and the Muses dwelled. The "mountain" in question was nothing more than a heap of earth from nearby quarries.

The romantic souls of those students may have given the quarter's development its first shot of adrenalin. As the 19th century dawned, cafes and entertainment spots began to proliferate in the area. Parisians began to arrive in throngs for a good evening's dance and general amusement. Though the "hill" was cleared away in the process, the name Montparnasse remained.

The golden years of Montparnasse were those between the two World Wars. Luminaries such as Modigliani, Chagall, Rilke, Max Jacob, Sartre, de Beauvoir, Cocteau, Guillaume Apollinaire, Stravinsky, Hemingway, Fitzgerald, Henry Miller and others sat, argued, ate, drank and fashioned a special ambience in the cafes and restaurants along bd. du Montparnasse.

By metro, get off at Vavin, Montparnasse-Bienvenue, or Edgar-Quinet. By bus, lines 91, 92, 94, 95, or 96.

Visit and rub shoulders with the "house celebrities" of the following establishments, which retain something of the atmosphere of yesteryear.

La Coupole, 102 bd. de Montparnasse, 14^{e}, tel. 43.20.14.20. Open daily till 1:45am, closed in August. *La Coupole* is a bar, restaurant, cafe, object of pilgrimage... and an inseparable part of 20th century Paris history. Since the 1920s, its red velvet seats, vast interior and illustrated ceiling dome have hosted an array of the famous people of the City of Lights.

La Coupole was not all glitter but rather a socio-intellectual rendezvous with a Bohemian touch and a charm which, though nearly inexplicable, persisted relentlessly, evening after evening.

Added to all was *La Coupole's* superb French cuisine and its rich and varied menu (not cheap but definitely not very expensive). The service used to be clockwork-efficient, classy and friendly, from the maitre d'hôtel to the cigarette girl.

One usually had to wait for a table in the evening. One place to wait was its bar. It, too, is a "historic site", enveloped in romantic tales (the poet Aragon met his Elsa here...). In light of all this, you can well understand why Parisians were enraged when, in 1987, René Lafonne, who had opened the restaurant 60 years previously, decided to sell the place — even if he was 90 years old by that time. The new manager, Jean Paul Bouche, appointed by the purchasing company, declared that the restaurant would be closed for a year to undergo renovations, which he stressed, would preserve all that was symbolic and of importance to the Parisians and their guests.

As promised the restaurant reopened in 1989, and it transpired that Bouche had remained true to his word — the place had been beautifully renovated and, remarkably, the charm maintained. It can still seat 600 diners, and is as full as ever every night. If you order reasonably, you can make out on 200f per person for dinner, which is not bad going if you consider that the story is free.

Businesspeople can now take advantage of *La Coupole*'s "Businessmen's Breakfast", which is intended only for them. An excellent breakfast includes omlettes with forest mushrooms. At your disposal is a telex, facsimile, photocopy machine, a telephone on the table and a messenger service.

La Closerie des Lilàs, 171 bd. de Montparnasse, 6e, tel. 43.26.70.50. Open daily 10:30am-2am. A piano bar and a restaurant, and in summer, a balcony swathed in greenery. Worth visiting for the original custom-mixed cocktails and, no less important, a glimpse of the impressive assortment of movie, TV and media stars who gather here regularly. Meals

MONTPARNASSE

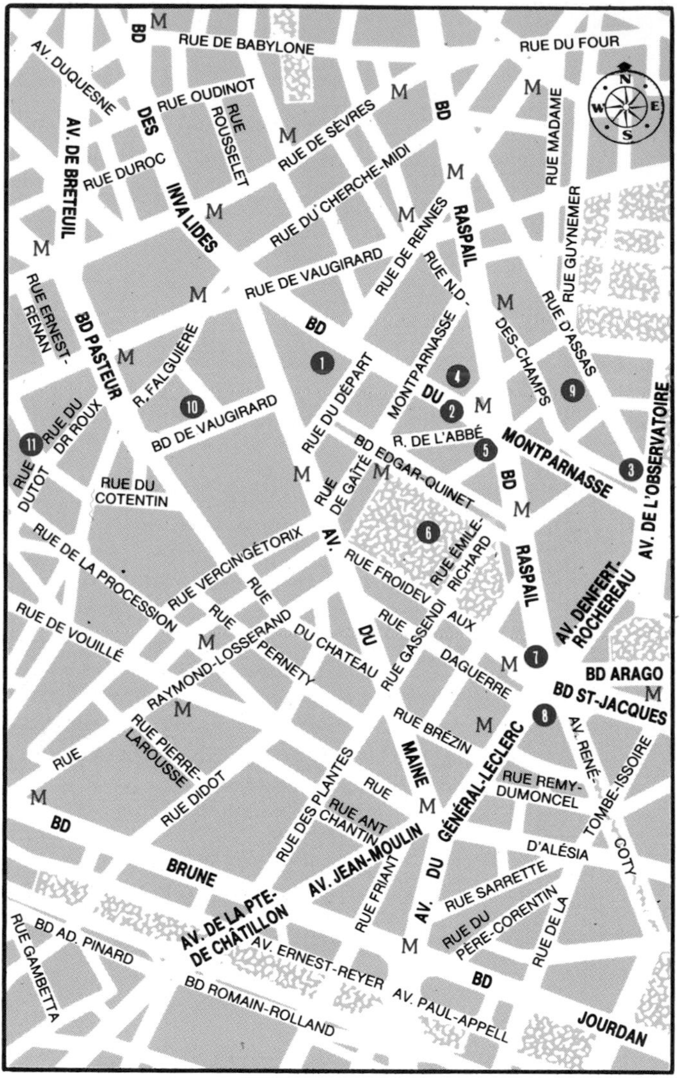

Index
1. Tour Montparnasse
2. La Coupole
3. La Closerie des Lilas
4. Le Sélect
5. Le Dôme
6. Cimetière Montparnasse (Montparnasse Cemetery)
7. Place Denfert Rochereau
8. Entrance to the Catacombes
9. Musée Zadkine
10. Musée de la Poste (Postal Museum)
11. Musée Pasteur

The Lion of Denfert-Rochereau

here tend to be expensive, around 300f per person, but it is certainly recommended for a drink.

Incidentally, *La Closerie* is not one of those places which time has eclipsed. It has always been a rendezvous of celebrities and celebrity-watchers. The names of some of its famous clients are engraved in the copper lining of the tables they once considered "theirs". One of these clients was a chap named Trotsky.

Another two establishments which merge a glorious past with an up-to-date reputations should be mentioned.

Le Dôme, 108 bd. de Montparnasse, 14e, tel. 43.35.34.82. Well known as a good restaurant and the regular watering hole of the famous couple Jean-Paul Sartre and Simone de Beauvoir. Today it specializes in sea food.

Le Sélect, 99 bd. de Montparnasse, 6e, a cafe which made its name as an international rendezvous of journalists and celebrities. Back when journalism was a more intimate profession, information was freely spread here.

Montparnasse still attracts quite a few artists and the glass-roofed upper stories of many of its houses shelter the studios of painters and sculptors. At first glance, this presence is less visible today than in past decades. The city's juggernaut development has taken its toll here, too. One of the major culprits is the skyscraper at the intersection of Bds. Montparnasse and Maine. A large commercial center on the lower levels draws throngs of shoppers, while its 59 floors are crammed with hundreds of offices. The new Montparnasse train station has also added to this change.

It is possible to ascend to the 56th floor of **Tour Montparnasse**, as this skyscraper is known, by special elevator. It zooms up in less than a minute. On a clear day, one can get an excellent panoramic view of Paris and outlying areas. There is also a special visitor's table to help with orientation. While upstairs, you can also see the small exhibition on the city.

One of the most interesting sites in the *quartier* is the famous **Cimetière Montparnasse**, 3 bd. Edgar-Quinet, 14e. Open daily 8am-5:30pm. The tombstones include quite a few genuine works of art. Some were the talk of the town in their time, such as *The Kiss* by Brancusi and another which depicts a man and woman in bed.

The men of renown buried here include Baudelaire, Maupassant, Saint-Saens, Soutine, and Sartre. Alfred Dreyfus, too, is interred in Montparnasse, not far from his defense counsel. The grave of the infamous Marshall Patan can also be seen here.

Boulevard Raspail runs to the north of the cemetery. It goes in a southerly direction to **Place Denfert-Rochereau**. The bronze lion which stands in the middle is intended to commemorate the bravery of Colonel Denfert-Rochereau's soldiers during the German invasion of 1870. On the left, opposite the metro entrance and the R.E.R., is the starting point of line 215, which goes to Orly Airport.

On the southern side of the plaza, stand two buildings opposite one another. The one on the left is the entrance to the **Catacombes**, tel. 43.22.47.63. Denfert-Rochereau metro station. Open Tues.-Fri. 2-4pm, Sat. and Sun. 9-11am and 2-4pm. Closed Monday. Entrance 13.5f.

This site should be omitted by those who are a little faint hearted or who recoil at anything connected to death. Here, one of death's underground sanctuaries is revealed. The illuminated trail, which is over one mile (1,800 m) long, is only a fraction of the huge space, consisting of numerous tunnels which were dug over hundreds of years ago — in the time of the Roman's — by the stone miners. The place got its macabre overtone towards the end of the 18th century, when the city authorities dug up all of Paris' cemeteries and transferred millions of skeletons and skulls to the catacombes. Since then, horrifying stories have been linked to the place, such as the festive balls which were held there by perverted noblemen (including Charles X), and the bands of criminals and rebels who found refuge in the gloomy caverns. On the other end of the scale, during the Nazi invasion of World War II, a commando unit of the underground was established in the catacombes.

Additional points of interest

Musée Zadkine, located at 100 rue d'Assas, tel. 43.26.91.90. Vavin metro station. Open daily 10am-5:40. Closed Monday. Entrance 10f. This is where the sculptor Zadkine lived and worked until his death in 1967. In addition to many of his works (from cubism to expressionism), the museum displays the sculptors' immediate environment, as it was when he was alive. Even his work apron is still hanging on the wall, as if Zadkine has just gone out for a glass of wine at the nearby cafe and is about to return to his work.

Musée de la Poste (The Postal Museum), at 34/35 bd. de Vaugirard, (north of the Montparnasse railway station), tel. 43.20.15.30. Montparnasse metro station. Open daily 10am-5pm. Closed Sunday. Entrance 10f.

In the fifteen exhibition halls of this lovely museum, the visitor gets a clear and comprehensive picture of everything connected to postal communications. The historical beginnings of the mail, the postal system of the Roman Empire through the Middle Ages, and its modern development, especially the technological advances. Of course, you can also see stamps and post boxes from different periods. Recommended, and not only for postmen and their families.

Musée Pasteur, 25 rue du Doctor-Roux, tel. 45.68.82.82. Pasteur metro station. Open daily 2-5:10pm. Closed Sat. and Sun. Entrance 10f. The name of Louis Pasteur, the great researcher, is, of course, familiar to everyone. Among his achievements was the development of a vaccine for rabies and the process of pasteurizing milk. There is a small museum, housed in the research center which bears his name, and you can also see the apartment in which he lived and the small church where he was buried. Exhibited in a special hall, are research and laboratory instruments from the past — from the days when a laboratory looked like a laboratory and not like a computer center.

Les Invalides — An Empire Remembered

Eglise du Dôme (Dome Church) is at the southern edge of the complex of buildings known as Les Invalides. Here, at the very bottom of six sarcophagi, one inside another, lies Emperor Napoléon Bonaparte, His remains were brought here in December 1840 from St. Hélène, the island on which he died in exile.

The aura of the diminutive Corsican who caused France to become a great empire still pervades. This area covers the western half of *Quartier* 7e and beyond. From the air, it would appear couched in the curve of the Seine.

Maubourg, La Tour, Varenne, Invalides, or Ecole Militaire metro stations. Bus, lines 28, 49, 69, 80, 82, 83, 87 or 92.

The block of buildings known as **Les Invalides** was erected in the second half of the 17th century, on the instruction of Louis XIV, as housing for disabled veterans. Its tenant population once reached some 6,000 veterans of the wars of France; some 100 disabled veterans still live here. The giant structure, whose facade runs for some 660 ft. (200 m), presently houses four museums and two churches. Next to Eglise du Dôme stands the Church of Saint-Louis, in which many of France's great generals are buried. The complex is located at 2 av. de Tourville.

Le Musée de l'Armée. Open daily 10am-5pm, summer till 6pm, tel. 45.55.92.30. The admission ticket (16f) is good for two days and allows entry to all the museums in the complex.

The museum, one of the largest of its type in the world, portrays the military history of France. Its exhibition halls display army flags, standards of army units as well as manikins of uniformed foot soldiers and horsemen with weapons from various periods — everything is life-size, including the horses.

The second-floor exhibit retells the victories and defeats of France throughout history, with special emphasis on the Napoleonic era. The Emperor's death mask and his room on

Ile St. Hélène, where he died in 1821, are reconstructed with precision.

Other halls house exhibits of the armies of François I and Henry IV and an impressive display of weapons and war material, knights' armor and uniforms from the 15th, 16th and 17th centuries. Of particular interest are the war instruments of famous personalities in the history of France. You can see the suit of armor which was worn by King Henry II, and the wonderfully crafted sword of King François I (1494-1547) which was raised to give the signal to the French army to begin the attack on the House of Habsburg in 1544.

The two World Wars (including the Allied landing on French shores) have a place of honor here as well. The inner court has an exhibit of artillery from its first timid booms on the battlefield to the modern era.

Musée des Plans-Reliefs. Open daily 10am-4:30pm, Oct.-March 10am-5:30pm. Models of cities and fortifications, once used for military strategic planning, are on display here. This was the passion of Louvois, Louis XIV's Minister of War, who brought this activity into vogue.

Musée de l'Ordre de la Libération. Open daily 2-5pm, closed Sun. and the month of August. The museum, in the western wing of Les Invalides and distinct from Musée de l'Armée, commemorates the guard of honor established by Général de Gaulle in honor of the Fighting Free French during the Nazi occupation. The museum tells the story in documents, photographs and mementos. There is a special section for the underground struggles and the Nazi death transports to the concentration and extermination camps.

Musée des Deux Guerres Mondiales. Open Tues.-Sat. 9am-5pm winter, 10am-6pm summer. The museum has a modest collection of mementos and documents from the two World Wars.

Les Invalides actually has two adjacent churches. One, **St.-Louis-des-Invalide**, was built for the resident disabled soldiers. Louis XIV decided that the place was not flashy enough. This explains the impressive dome and the neo-classical columns around it.

Napoléon is buried here, though not alone; his son, the king of Rome, is interred beside him, and his two brothers Joseph and Jerome rest a little farther away. They were kings of Spain and Westphalia, respectively. Marshalls Foch and Lyautey had the honor of being buried here as well.

At the western end of the Les Invalides complex, at the corner of bd. des Invalides and rue Varenne, is a museum devoted to one of the greatest, and certainly the best-known French sculptor, Rodin. It is located in Hôtel Biron, a mansion dating from the early 18th century. One of the owners of this house was Marshall De Biron, son to a family of esteemed army commanders. **Musée Rodin**, 77 rue de Varenne, tel. 47.05.01.34. Open daily 10am-5:15pm; closed Tues. Admission fee.

Its sixteen exhibition halls display a comprehensive compendium of artwork, including Rodin's world-famous masterpieces: *The Thinker*, *The Burghers of Calais*, *The Kiss* and *Gate of Hell*. Other works are set in the beautiful palace gardens, impressive to visit in their own right. Among other exhibits, you can see the earliest works of the artist and the sketches which he prepared for his sculptures. The museum also exhibits works of other artists, including the famous Norwegian painter Edvard Munch, Van Gogh, Renoir and Monet.

Once we are already in rue Verenne, we can deviate slightly to the east and walk down to **Hôtel de Matignon**, which is to the right immediately after rue Vaneau. This palace was named after its first tenant, the Duchess De Matignon. Towards the second half of the 18th century, it became famous when it was bought by Talleyrand, the renowned politician who also served as Napoléon's Minister of Foreign Affairs and who played a key role in the Vienna Congress of 1815. Since the 1950s, the palace has served as the official residence of the prime minister of France.

Returning to Les Invalides, behind it, rue Lowendal leads to the front of yet another complex. **l'Ecole Militaire**, the grand academy of war, has produced the commanders of the French army ever since its establishment under Louis XV. One can sense its mass and power just by walking around it.

Since it is a military installation, l'Ecole is not easy to visit. Those who insist, assuming they have a good reason, can put in a written request. The address: l'Ecole Militaire, 1 Place Joffre, Direction Generale, Paris, 75007.

Index

1. Les Invalides
2. Eglise du Dôme
3. Musée Rodin
4. Ecole militaire
5. Champ de Mars
6. Tour Eiffel
7. Jardins de Chaillot
8. Palais de Chaillot
9. Pont Alexandre III (Alexandre III Bridge)
10. Petit Palais
11. Grand Palais (Museum of the Discovery)
12. Rond-Point des Champs-Elysées
13. Stamp market
14. La Boutique à Sandwiches

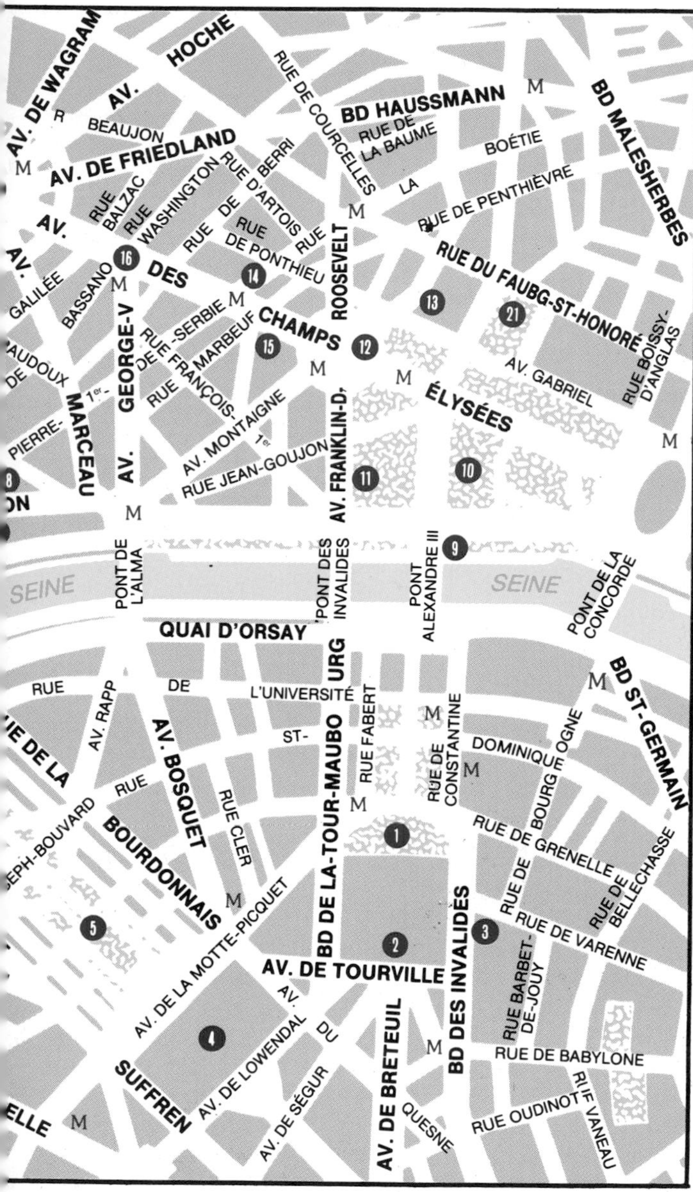

15. L'Alsace
16. Les Champs-Elysées
17. Arc de Triomphe
18. Musée de la Mode et du Costume (Palais Galliéra)
19. Musée d'Art Moderne de la Ville de Paris
20. Musée Guimet
21. Palais de l'Elysée

The open space northwest of L'Ecole Militaire, a landscaped and well-tended area used to be the army's parade and line-up grounds. Hence its name, **Champ-de-Mars** (Champ meaning field, Mars meaning war, a reference to the Roman god of war). Between its first designation and today's, was a period in which it was used for mass events. In 1783, for example, the very first balloon was launched here. Popular festivities were held in this field, as were, of course, the great international expositions of 1867, 1878 and 1889. There is also the strange and controversial structure that was erected for the 1889 exposition — the Eiffel Tower.

La Tour Eiffel

Despite all development since the 1889 International Exposition, La Tour Eiffel is still the highest observation point in Paris at 1,050 ft. (320 m, including the TV antenna). It is also the emblem of the French capital and an attraction which draws more than 4 million visitors each year. The tower was recently renovated, reinforced and cleaned. Its third story was reopened to visitors.

The tower's origins may now be obscure to many who climb it. The organizers of the 1889 International Exposition wanted to mark the centennial of the Revolution with an extraordinary monument. Of the hundreds of competing proposals submitted, some were rather ridiculous. Someone suggested building a giant guillotine tens of feet high in memory of the casualties... Someone else proposed a pillar 660 ft. (220 m) tall, crowned with a mighty lamp capable of illuminating all of Paris. One engineer even envisioned a mammouth fountain which would spray refreshing water on the city on hot summer days. In the end, engineer Gustav Eiffel's plan for a tower of metal elements was selected and adopted. The total weight of his tower: 7,300 tons (with the latest additions, the weight now reaches some 10,000 tons).

The decision triggered a public tempest which will never be forgotten. A large body of Parisians and men of letters demanded that the tower project be scrapped for the irreparable eyesore it would produce. But, in January 1887 work on the foundations were begun, reaching a depth of 45 ft. (14 m). Thereafter, the actual construction work commenced, the hammers clinked away, the welders sent sparks flying and the tower was completed on schedule.

A few pertinent features of this Parisian giant: The tower is constructed from 15,000 metal pieces which are held together by two-and-a-half million iron brackets. A crew of 50 engineers and draftsmen prepared 5,300 sketches for its construction, which required 250 workers to execute. For those fit sportsmen who wish to forego use of the elevator — there are 1,710 steps to climb to the third floor. Painting the tower (it is done every seven years) requires 40,000 work hours and 45 tons of paint. On particularly hot days, when the metal of the Eiffel Tower expands, the tower can "grow" by almost half a foot (15 cm).

Its dedication was greeted with a 21-gun salute. All this merely fueled the controversy which has polarized Paris into pro-tower and anti-tower factions. The exposition over petitions in favor of destroying the tower proliferated and, in 1910, plans were made to dismantle it. Ironically, the salvation of the Eiffel Tower came in the midst of World War I when it served as an important radio-telegraph center for the French General Headquarters. In June 1949, television antennae were attached to the top of the tower, and so France was able to see its first televised news broadcast. Its final and official seal of approval came in January 1964 when the Government of France declared it a national site.

The tower has three floors, each offers a panoramic view and other attractions. Open 10:30am-11pm, from 9:30am in summer. The first floor is 186 ft (57 m) high. The stairs go as high as the second floor (no easy proposition even to the first floor, but it can be done). There is an admission fee for both stairs and the elevator. On this level there are souvenier shops, a restaurant, cafe and fast-food establishment; a cinema devoted to the Tower's history; a post office (open daily 10:30am-7:30pm) with an exclusive concession on stamps labelled *La Tour Eiffel — Paris*, a branch of the city's tourist office (which is open May-Sept.), a counter for moneychanging, and a room which can be reserved for special events.

The second floor is 426 ft. (130 m) above street level (the price of the elevator also goes up). Here you can find shops,

The view from the Eiffel Tower

a gallery and the opulent *Restaurant Jules Verne* which adds a prestige menu to the view. Sample prices: 500f per person; 230f for a fixed-price menu (only for lunch on weekdays). Reservations are recommended, tel. 45.55.61.44. A special rapid private elevator is placed at the clientele's disposal.

The third floor, about 985 ft. (300 m) up, provides you with a panoramic view of a huge expanse of the city, with explanations at a special table. Here, too, is **Salon Tour Eiffel** — the office Gustav Eiffel built for himself, which he used until his death in 1923 at the age of 91.

At ground level, near the western leg of the tower, is the elevator engine room which may be visited. The wonderful engines, installed in 1899, look as if they had been taken from a science-fiction movie of the early cinema age — no coincidence, perhaps.

Climb down from the Eiffel Tower and cross the Seine on Pont d'Iéna (to the northwest) through Warsaw Plaza to **Jardins de Chaillot**. Its slopes are the favored surfaces

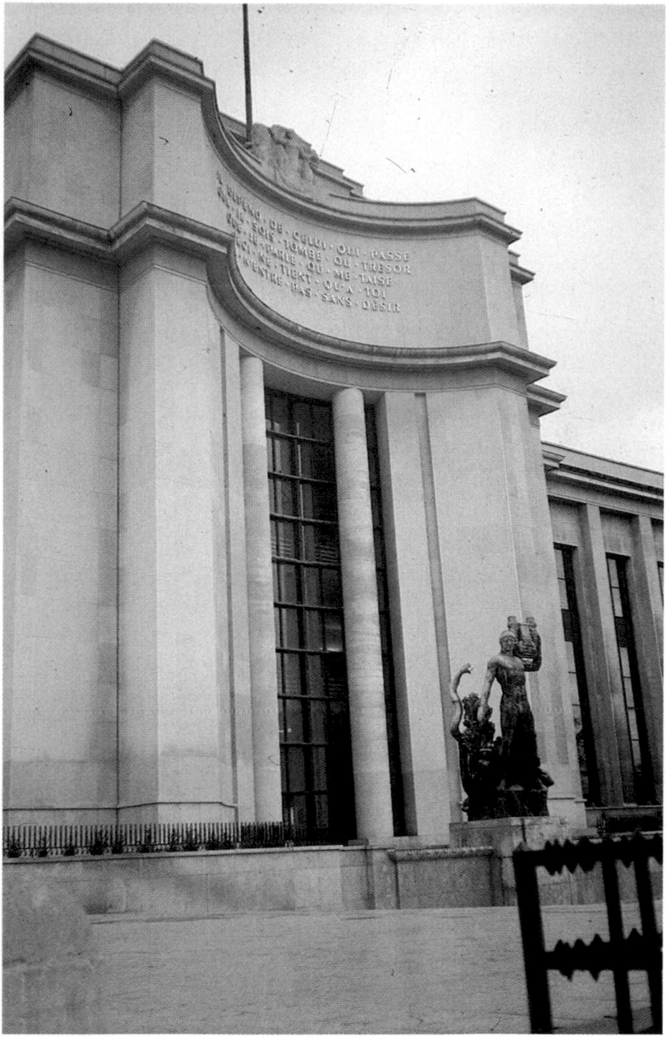

Palais de Chaillot

for young Parisians who spend their weekends stunting on skates and skateboards, a parade which sometimes makes parking difficult. The twin wings of Palais de Chaillot seem to gaze down on the park. Climb up to its balconies for a wonderful view — the park, the fountains, the Seine, the Eiffel Tower, Champ de Mars... as far as L'Ecole Militaire. The view is equally splendid at night, when you can see the special lighting which has been installed.

The massive structure, built for the 1937 World's Fair, today houses the Chaillot National Theater (its auditorium stretches below the compound between the two wings), as well as four museums.

Musée de l'Homme (Museum of Mankind), in the western wing, tel. 45.53.70.60. Open daily 9:45am-5:15pm, closed Tues. Admission fee. The museum has a fascinating exhibit of the history and development of mankind, various civilizations and their art (prehistory, anthropology and ethnology). One of the most famous exhibits here is an Incan mummy from South America. Part of the museum is devoted to the technological development of various societies worldwide. The museum also presents changing exhibitions on related themes.

Musée de la Marine (Maritime Museum), also in the western wing, tel. 45.53.31.70. Open daily 10am-6pm, closed Tues. and holidays. Admission fee. This museum is devoted to French and general maritime affairs with regard to their history, art, science, technology and traditions. It also has a splendid collection of model ships, including history-making vessels such as the one in which America was discovered, Christopher Columbus' Santa Maria.

Musée des Monuments Français, in the northern wing, tel. 47.27.35.74. Open daily 9:45am-12:30pm and from 2-5:15pm, closed Tues. Admission fee. Once a museum of sculpture, its name and purpose were changed in 1937. Collectors began to assemble a stunning inventory of perfect replicas (in plaster, clay and other materials) of the most famous monuments in France. Visitors who do not intend to explore the entire country in depth can form a good impression of the treasures of architecture and art outside Paris right here.

Musée du Cinéma, also in the northern wing, tel. 45.53.74.39. Open daily, closed Tues. Guided tours only: 10am, 11am, 2pm, 3pm and 4pm. Admission fee. This institution, near the **Cinémathèque Française**, spans nearly 100 years of cinema art. It provides a view behind the scenes of the world of illusion — actors, props, cameras — from the origins of the art to our own time. For confirmed cinema lovers, the exhibit includes Valentino's robe from *Son of the Sheik* and a robot from Fritz Lang's *Metropolis.*

Chaillot fountains — a view towards the Eiffel Tower

Place de la Concorde

Pont Alexandre III

Champs-Elysées — Opulence and More Opulence

When the Nazis entered Paris in June 1940, they made their conquest official with a showy parade down Avenue des Champs-Elysées. From that moment until the end of the occupation, the Germans sent a military honor guard parading down the avenue every day to demonstrate that they were in charge.

By so doing, they were, in a sense, exploiting the symbolic significance of this avenue for Paris, France and the world. Champs-Elysées is emblematic of the pride and prestige which Général Charles de Gaulle restored and fortified the day the city was liberated. He returned to Paris on August 26, 1945, in a parade down Champs-Elysées, of course.

The 1.2 mile (2 km) concourse traverses the southern section of *Quartier 8*, between Place de la Concorde and Place de l'Etoile-Charles de Gaulle. It has two sections, each different in nature.

The eastern section, between Place de la Concorde and Rond-Point-des-Champs-Elysées, is lined with theaters, museums, restaurants and various gaudy structures in a setting of landscaped, green open space. The studios of the second television network are also situated here. On the northern side of the landscaped area are Palais de l'Elysées, the official residence of the President of France, as well as the American and British Embassies.

The second section, between the Rond-Point and l'Etoile, is the district where the prestige, glory, opulence and elegance of Champs-Elysées is kept alive. It abounds with cinemas, luxury shops, classy cafes and fancy restaurants. All this leads to Place de l'Etoile. Parisians still insist on referring to it as such although it officially took on the name of Charles de Gaulle following his death. Twelve boulevards set out in all directions from the plaza. In the middle is the great Arc de Triomphe; to its south is *Quartier 16*ᵉ, Paris' ritzy residential quarter.

Champs-Elysées is reached by metro — from east to west; Champs-Elysées, Clémenceau, Franklin D. Roosevelt, Georges V, Charles de Gaulle-Etoile and bus lines 31, 32, 42, 73, 80.

The green triangle south of Champs-Elysées (between the boulevard and the Seine) near Place de la Concorde, owes much of its beauty and impressiveness to the great World's Fair held in Paris in 1900.

Study the Left Bank at the **Palais Bourbon** section, noting the Palace itself (home of the French National Assembly) and the edge of the vast Les Invalides plaza. Pont Alexandre III, Paris' widest bridge, and one of its loveliest, leads from here to the Right Bank of the Seine. It was built for the 1900 exposition, its cornerstone laid by the visiting Crown Prince of Russia, who later became Czar Nicholas II. The bridge is named after his father. The statues at each of the four corners of the bridge symbolize different periods in French history: the Middle Ages and the Modern Era stand on the Right Bank; the Renaissance and Imperial periods on the Left.

Across the bridge to the right, on Avenue Winston Churchill, is another memento of the 1900 fair. It is **Le Petit Palais**, the "little palace", a handsome specimen of the architecture of its time. Today it houses the Municipal Museum of Fine Arts, tel. 42.65.12.73. Open daily 10am-5:40pm. Closed Mon. Admission 9f.

The impressive collections in Le Petit Palais include ancient Egyptian and Greek sculpture, Renaissance art, sculpture and furnishings, medieval manuscripts, Dutch and Flemish art from the 16th and 17th centuries and 19th and early 20th century French painting, including works by Bonnard, Pissarro, Manet, Monet, Courbet, Corot and Delacroix. Frequently changing exhibits on different themes are on display as well.

Across from Le Petit Palais is **Le Grand Palais**, it, too, a relic of the 1900 exposition. Its northern and middle sections are generally used for large exhibits, as well as antique markets, book fairs and more.

The eastern wing, in the direction of Avenue Franklin D. Roosevelt, is **Palais de la Découverte** (The Museum of

Palais Bourbon — seat of the National Assembly

Discovery). Open daily 10am-6pm, closed Mon. Admission 11f (add 10f for admission to planetarium).

The trail-blazing experiments of Galileo, Newton, Leonardo da Vinci and others are performed regularly in this museum, which aims to document the development of scientific research. The halls progress thematically: Biology in the Service of Man, Electricity, Nuclear Physics, Laser Beams, and so on. The displays are specially designed to whet the curiosity and interest of visitors regarding the development of science and research. The new planetarium on the grounds has a dome almost 50 ft. (15 m) in diameter, and seating for 300 people.

On exiting the museum, turn right into av. Franklin Roosevelt, past the **Rond-Point Theater**, until the Rond-Point-des-Champs-Elysées Plaza, to the greenish glass fountains which surround it. North-east of the plaza, at **Carré Marigny**, there awaits any philatelist, past or present, an amusing and fun experience. This is the site of the stamp market, and here you can see dozens of traders dealing in stamps from all over the world, either from suitcases or proper booths. For the most part there are no bargains, and most dealers are equipped with thick catalogs listing the price of the stamps

Arc de Triomphe

The market operates three days a week: Thursday, Saturday and Sunday, from 10am-6pm. Return to the plaza and head west back to the Champs-Elysées.

Continue down Champs-Elysées about 220 yards (200 m) after the Rond-Point (toward Place de l'Etoile) and turn right on rue Colisée. At No. 12, is a boisterous establishment which can always raise a smile — *La Boutique à Sandwichs*, tel. 43.59.56.69. Worth a visit to relax and sample the tasty offerings.

The ground-floor shop serves a large selection of the best sandwiches in Paris at reasonable prices (the upper story is a proper restaurant). You can either order take-aways or eat there. Open till 1am, closed Sun. During the lunch hour, *La Boutique* fills up with an impressive pantheon of people who look like a *Who's Who* catalogue even when they're not.

For those wanting a more "serious" meal, cross the road to *L'Alsace*, a virtual temple for lovers of the famous Alsacian delicacy *sauerkraut* (slightly sour spiced cabbage embellished with various cold cuts). It is located at 39 Champs-Elysées, tel. 43.59.44.24. Open 24-hours daily. Experts rank its *sauerkraut* right at the top. The decor is beautiful and entertaining, and the local beer, *Blancs D'Alsace* deserves special citation. Open every day around the clock, fixed-price menu: 250f.

There are several other stops of interest along the Champs-Elysées. At No. 52-60, is a rare gem of a shop called *Virgin Megastore* — paradise for anyone looking for records, compact disks, videos, etc. The prices are reasonable and there are even some bargains. Further on, at No. 99, is *Fouquets*, one of the finest and best known restaurants in the city. It's the popular gathering place of film stars and their directors, but "regular mortals" can also enter and go upstairs to the top floor lounges with magnificent, though somewhat ostentatious, decor or sit on the ground floor terraces which overlook the boulevard. A fixed-price menu costs about 200f per person, but this can be double or more if you order a la carte. You must not overlook the establishment located at No. 116 — namely *Le Lido*, arguably the world's most famous night club, renowned for its cabaret shows.

Continue down until the end of Champs-Elysées to the magnificent **Place de L'Etoile** (Star Plaza), known officially as Place Charles de Gaulle since 1970. The plaza acquired its present configuration in 1854, eighteen years after **Le Grand Arc de Triomphe** was completed.

As for the Arc, "grand" is the right word. At 150 ft. (45 m) wide and 160 ft. (49 m) high, it is the largest monument of its kind in the world. Construction began in 1806 by order of Napoléon Bonaparte as a memorial to his victories. When the Empire fell in 1815, however, work on the Arc stopped, resuming only by order of Louis XVIII seven years later. Many artists of the period, such as Rude, donated their talents to the project, commemorating scenes of heroism from French history in sculpture and stone relief. Each "tooth" in the serrated embellishment at the top of the arch is devoted to a triumph of Napoléon's armies

Interestingly, the sun sets exactly through the opening of L'Arc de Triomphe on December 2, the anniversary of the Battle of Austerlitz. Coincidental...

The **Tomb of the Unknown Soldier** was relocated to this site in 1921. Since then, official memorial ceremonies have been held here.

Climb the Arc, and enjoy the view. In order to reach the Arc de Triomphe, do not cross the plaza, but rather use the underground passage leading from the stairs on the right end of the Champs-Elysées. You can use either the elevator or the stairs to reach the top of the Arc, where you can take advantage of the splendid view and take in a film on the Arc's history. Open daily 10am-6pm, winter only until 4pm. Every day at 6:30pm you can watch the ceremony of the lighting of the flame for the Unknown Soldier.

Additional points of interest

There is no more suitable place than Paris for this museum: **Musée de la Mode et du Costume**. In Palais Galliéra, just off Champs-Elysées at 10 Avenue Pierre de Serbie, 16e, tel. 47.20.85.46. léna or Alma-Marceau metro stations. Open Mon.-Sat. 10am-5:30pm. Admission 12f.

Palais Galliéra, built by the Duchess of Galliéra in the late 19th century, houses an extraordinary collection of some 4,000 full costumes and another 25,000 articles of women's, men's and children's clothing dating from 1735 to our time. Though the exhibit covers the entire social spectrum, the showpiece is the opulent attire of the wealthy. It includes the wardrobes of famous women in French history.

A natural extension of a visit to the fashion museum is a tour of the northern part of *Quartier 16e*, between Place de l'Etoile and Place Trocadéro and the area south of the Champs-Elysées, av. Montaigne. The area proliferates with top fashion and elite designers. All the fashion creations of the truly great names, Dior, Yves Saint-Laurent, Nina Ricci, begin here.

Next to Palais Galliéra, to the south, is **le Musée d'Art Moderne de la Ville de Paris** (the Museum of Modern Art of the City of Paris). The museum, located at 11 av. Du President Wilson, presents its permanent collection as well

Champs-Elysées

as changing exhibitions. Open daily 10am-5:40pm, Wed. until 8:30pm. Closed Monday. Entrance to the permanent collection free.

Here you can see works of better-known artists from the present century, who represent different streams in modern art. Among them are works by Braque, Picasso, Vlaminck, Vassarely, Agam, Laisse, Soutine, Chagall and others. Raoul Dufy's huge *Electric Fairy* stands out among the artistic works — it measures almost 200 ft. by 32 ft. (60 m x 10 m). Matisse's triptych *The Dance* is another particularly noteworthy piece. The extremely popular fourth floor of the museum is an exciting place to see experimental arts in different spheres — from photography to music.

There is another museum right next door — **Musée Guimet** at 6 Place d'léna, tel. 47.23.61.65. Open daily 9:45am-5:10pm. Closed Tuesday. Entrance 15f. Like others of its kind, this museum has the familiar beginnings of a wealthy man, in this case Emile Guimet, who went on a trip to Asia, became enamoured with the art and returned home with a substantial collection. Towards the end of the 19th century, his splendid collection formed the basis of the museum, which was given over to the state. Today, it is one of the greatest museums in Europe dealing in Asian art. Included among the exhibits are art and *objets d'art* from Nepal, Vietnam, Tibet, Java Islands, Afganistan, Pakistan and China. It provides a very interesting trip into the spirit of the Far East, to its mystery and strangeness, from the European perspective. Once at the museum do not miss seeing the jewel of the collection on the first floor: a statue of the dancing god Shiva, which is 900 years old and astonishingly beautiful.

L'Opéra and Cash Registers

In the southwestern section of Quartier 9, between l'Opéra and the Trinite Church, is Paris' frenetic, bustling, picturesque shopping district. In its very center are two of the best-known department stores of all: *Galeries Lafayette* and *le Printemps*.

Take the metro to Auber or l'Opéra, or bus 20, 22, 52, 53, 66 or 95.

This area took on its present color during the bustling years of Baron Haussmann, Prefect of the Seine District under Napoleon III. It was Haussmann's idea to make space for Place de l'Opéra and pave Avenue de l'Opéra and other streets in the *quartier*. Construction of Gare St.-Lazare gave Paris another reason to choose this area as its financial and commercial center.

The *quartier's* second personality is represented by the opera house, the well-known **Olympia Performance Center** and **la Bibliothéque Nationale**, at the eastern fringe of the district.

L'Opéra de Paris is open to visitors on weekdays, 11am-4:30pm. Owing to various events, such as rehearsals and auditions, it is best to inquire in advance about touring the building, tel. 42.66.50.22 or 47.42.57.50.

A side entrance from 1 Place Charles Garnier leads to the small **Opera House Museum.** Open daily 10am-5pm, closed Sun. Admission 6f. The museum has paintings of some of the greats who composed for, sang or danced on the Opera stage. You can also see Debussy's desk, Nijinsky's dancing shoes, a head ornament which belonged to the great dancer Anna Pavlova and miniature models of sets from the operas staged here.

The opera building, designed by architect Charles Garnier, is an exceptional example of the style of Napoléon III's Second Empire period. It took ten years, 1862-1872, to erect this impressive hall. The result was an almost impossible eclectic of marble ramps, statues, sculptured balustrades, insets, columns, crystal chandeliers, and carvings in stone and copper. The opulence and colors of the hall itself are extraordinary. Observe the velvet, the gold, the balconies, the mysteriously deep private boxes, and a relatively new embellishment, the Marc Chagall ceiling, which was added in 1964.

The opera is enjoying a great revival in Paris these days. Thousands of admirers throng the opera house and tickets are usually hard to obtain. Reservations are recommended. Prices: 40-440f. In answer to this great demand, the new Opéra de la Bastille was opened in 1989.

Behind the opera house, at 40 bd. Haussmann, is the large department store which has become synonymous with exclusive shopping — **Galeries Lafayette**. An exit from the Chaussée d'Antin metro station leads directly to its basement. Inside, after scanning the tremendous inventory of fashion goods, cosmetics, housewares and just about any item imaginable, stop for a moment in the center of the ground floor and glance upward. The impressive dome of the building evokes a temple — of consumerdom...

At the end of rue Chaussée-d'Antin is the Ste.-Trinité church, built in the Second Empire style characteristic to the neighborhood. Its small garden is a fine place for a rest after shopping.

Le Printemps, the second great department store, is next to *Galeries Lafayette* at 64 bd. Haussmann. Apart from its generally impressive dimensions, its spice department is Europe's largest and its upper-floor restaurant offers a splendid view of Paris.

From the bd. Haussmann exit of *le Printemps*, cross the boulevard to reach the Paris branch of **Marks and Spencer** at No. 35. This establishment is noteworthy for a richly appointed department of English foods. For visitors who crave something British during their visit to Paris, here's the place.

Continuing west on bd. Haussmann, on your left you will see a little garden, named for Louis VI. In the center of the garden stands a small church which has an interesting history. In 1793, when Louis XVI and his wife, Marie Antoinette were beheaded, they were interred next to the wall of what was then the Madeleine cemetery. They were buried in unmarked graves. In 1815, however, when Louis XVIII ascended the

THE OPERA

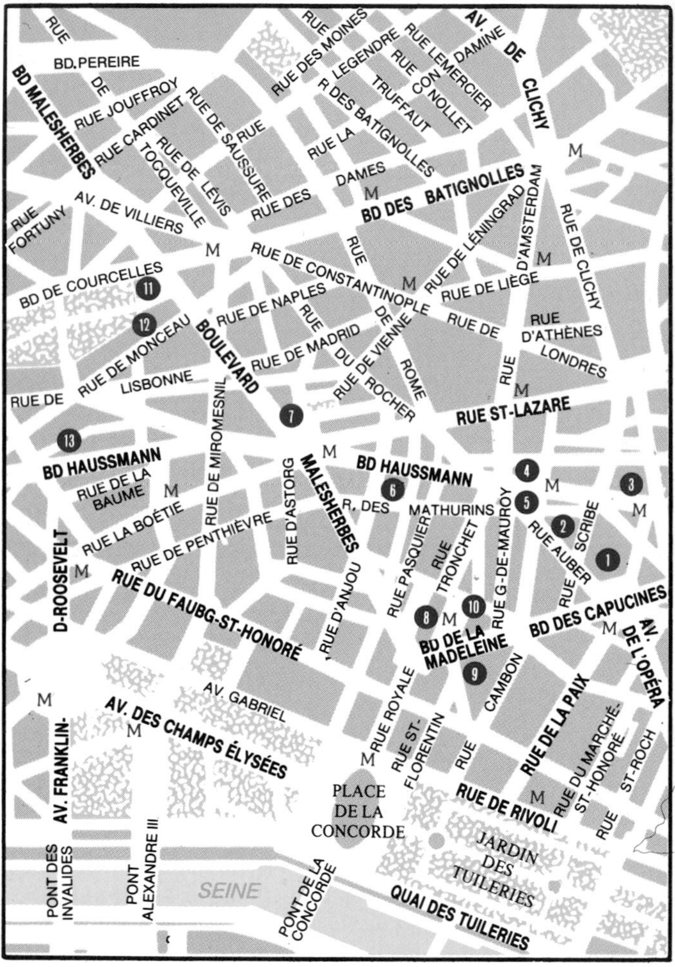

index

1. Opera House
2. Opera House Museum
3. Galeries Lafayette
4. Le Printemps
5. Marks and Spencer
6. Jardin de Louis XVI
7. Eglise St. Augustin
8. Church of the Madeleine
9. Aux Trois Quartiers
10. Fauchon
11. Musée Cernushi
12. Musée Nissim de Camondo
13. Musée Jacquemart-André

L'Opéra

Eglise de la Trinité

throne, he demanded that the body of his brother and sister-in-law be exhumed. The task took several days before the remains were located. The unfortunate couple were then given a honorable burial, with full ceremony, at the **Basilica of St.-Denis**, near Paris.

Louis XVIII then decreed that a church be built in the area of the original graves. The task was entrusted to Fontaine, who had served as Napoleon's architect. The church took eleven years until completed, by which time Charles X was the ruling monarch. The structure, in neo-classical style, is open daily to visitors, from 10am-6pm during the summer, and until 5pm in winter.

Continue along the boulevard until you reach St.-Augustin plaza, which stands in the shadow of the **St.-Augustin Church**. This impressive edifice was built in Italian rennaisance style by the architect Butler, during the reign of Napoleon the Third.

A left turn into bd. Malesherbes, another of the roads paved by Baron Haussmann, leads on to the **Church of Madeleine**, just between Quartiers 8 and 9. Open daily 7:30am-7pm, tel. 42.65.52.17.

The church, shaped like a classical Greek temple on a massive scale, underwent a lengthy and painful birth. Construction began in 1764 but was interrupted by the Revolution. While debating whether to designate it as a theater or as a bank, the new regime let the time pass. Napoléon, after crowning himself emperor, decided to make it a "temple of glory" for the great French army. After his empire fell, Louis XVIII redesignated it as a church, and a church it has remained. The Church of the Madeleine, with its 52 impressive Corinthian columns, each 66 ft. (20 m) high, was consecrated in 1842.

The lavishly embellished interior is crowned by three domes through which the rays of sun penetrate. The church is decorated with works such as *the Ascension of Madeleine*,and *the Baptism of Jesus* by Rude. Monthly concerts of church music are held here.

Next to the church, on the northeast corner is a delicatessen of well-earned fame. It is *Fauchon*, the glory of Paris delicatessens, with a tremendous selection of more than 20,000 varieties of food, fruit, vegetables, wines, baked goods and more. Enter, sniff and (budget permitting) taste. *Fauchon* is also a self-service restaurant. The menu which includes fantastic sandwiches (27f), superb quiche (26f), Italian-style dumplings (34f) and dozens of varieties of cakes, compensates for the crowding and noise. Open 9:45am-6:30pm, closed Sun.

Between the church and the delicatessen there is a small flower market in a greenhouse-like structure. On the corner opposite *Fauchon* stands its serious competitor, *Hédiard*, which is also an excellent delicatessen.

At the southeastern corner of Place de Madeleine is another large department store, *Aux Trois Quartiers*, with an exceptional selection of classical fashion. It is the favorite of the Paris aristocracy — and its imitators.

Additional points of interest

At the point where we turned left in the direction of the Church of Madeleine, we could have rather turned right onto bd. Malesherbes, which would lead us to two museums. A third museum can be reached by way of St.-Augustin plaza, though bd. Haussmann.

Musée Cernuschi, at 7 Av. Valeasques, 8e, tel. 45.63.50.75. Monceau metro station. Open daily 10am-5:40pm, closed Monday. The museum is devoted to Chinese art, and started out as the private collection of the wealthy banker Henri Cernuschi. His special love of the Orient sent him on a long trip to China during the second half of the 19th century. He returned laden with valuables, works of art and antiques dating back as far as 300 BC. Items such as decorated bowls and jars, and ceramic and bronze utensils reflect the dominant artistic culture of the Chinese dynasties during various periods. Paricularly noteworthy, is the collection of dolls from the Thang Dynasty and the painted silk screens. In 1896, the museum fell under the auspices of the municipality of Paris, since which time many other exhibits have been added to the collection.

Musée Nissim de Camondo, 63 rue de Monceau, 8e, tel. 45.63.26.32. Monceau metro station. Open daily 10am-12pm, 2-5pm. Closed Monday and Tuesday. At the turn of the century, the Baron Moise de Camondo, built himself a castle in the style of the Petit Trianon at Versailles. He filled the

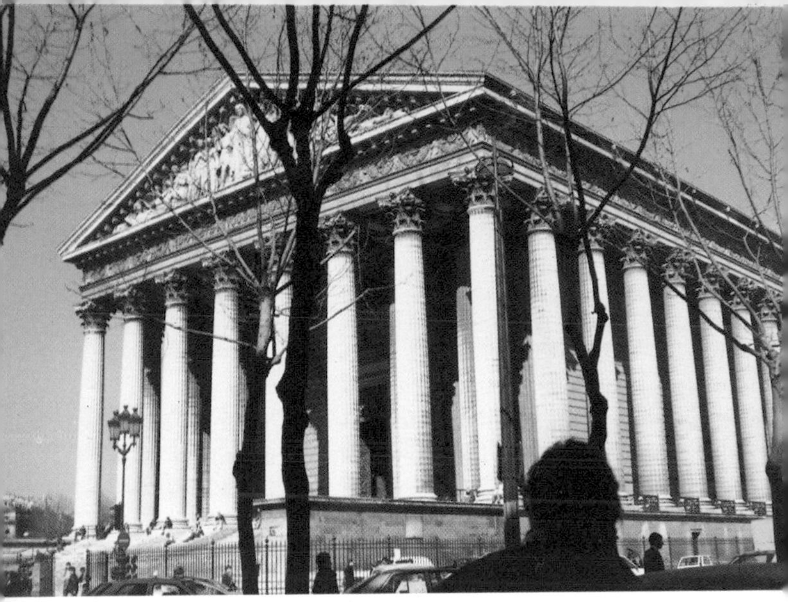

La Madeleine

Rue Royale — between the Madeleine and Place de la Concorde

many rooms and halls with his family's large collection of art works. When his son Nissim, a pilot in the French air force, was killed in an air combat during World War I, the baron decided to establish a special memorial monument in his name. He tranferred ownership of the castle, with its large collection of art, to the Authority of Museums and Decorative Arts in Paris.

Visitors to the museum are transported back in time and can get a real picture of how the aristocracy lived in the 18th century. Their furniture, the art and the absolute luxury all bear testimony to a by-gone era. The Camondo family, particularly the Baron Moïse, acquired some of the finest examples of 18th French carpentry, as well as paintings and sculptures from that period. Everything has been preserved and tended with much care and devotion over many years. A highly recommended experience.

Musée Jacquemart-André, 158 bd. Haussmann, 8e, tel. 45.62.39.94. St.-Philippe du Roule metro station. This museum houses works of art, from a rich collection which was assembled in the latter half of the 19th century by a collector-couple, Edward André Jacquemart and his wife Nellie. Most of the art was acquired during their trips to Europe, particularly Italy, on which they embarked for this very purpose. Their collection includes works by Donatello, Della Robbia, Botticelli, Bosch, Frans Hals and Fragonard. The museum also schedules changing exhibitions. The museum was temporarily closed in 1989, and those wishing to visit should call tel. 42.89.04.91 for an up-date regarding visiting.

La Bibliothèque Nationale (the National Library) at 58 rue de Richelieu 2e, tel. 42.61.82.83. Bourse or Pyramides metro stations. Admission 10f.

The building was originally erected for Cardinal Mazarin, and some sections were subsequently converted into a royal library by Louis XV and, later still, into a national library. The Bibliothèque houses one of the world's largest collections of books, manuscripts, printed writings and engravings. Since 1537, the library has taken in every book published in France and its total collection now exceeds six million volumes. One needs to make arrangements in advance to explore the books, but the public may observe the size and beauty of the Second Empire-style reading hall through its glass doors.

The first floor of the library houses an exhibition of medallions, decorations, silver coins and antiquities. Open Mon.-Fri., 1-5pm.

Not far from L'Opéra at 25 bd. des Capucines, 2e, stood Musée Cognacq-Jay, but it closed down towards the latter part of 1988. The museum is now to be housed in the Donnon Palace.

Look left and right from Place de l'Opéra. To the right is one of Paris' most elegant and famous café-restaurants, *Café de la Paix*. To the left is what was once *Le Drugstore*, but today is simply a complex of little shops for food, gifts, periodicals, books, electronics, cigarettes, tobacco, records, video tapes, etc.

Montmartre — The Rise and Fall of a Hill

The story of this hill reads somewhat like a biography of a country girl who heads for the big time and ends up in the gutter. The hill-hero in this case (*La Butte* to its local friends), known officially as Montmartre, has a fascinating and instructive story to tell. As in all such tales, it has a rather unhappy ending.

The name Montmartre originates in a dramatic and miraculous event involving St. Denis, the man who brought Christianity to Paris. In 250 AD, as pagan Rome pursued the disciples of Jesus, St. Denis was sentenced to be beheaded. After "justice" was done, Christian tradition relates, the holy man bent over, picked up his head and carried it to this hill north of town. He later continued on to the site now known as St.-Denis. Ever since, the hill has been known as "Montmartyre" — Mount of the Martyr. The present spelling is only a slight distortion.

A tranquil, quiet village rested on the hill and its flanks for hundreds of years. Some of its residents grew grapes and produced wine; others tended the windmills (which numbered 30 at their peak) and provided flour for nearby Paris.

Two concurrent developments in the late 19th century upset the pastoral serenity of Montmartre. First, Paris grew and expanded, its northern border encompassing the hilltop village. Second, painters, sculptors, authors, poets, musicians and artists of other stripes discovered the area and gradually began migrating there, making it their home.

Paris' nightlife and entertainment district developed at the foot of the southern flank of the hill. Nightclubs with bouncing can-can dancers sprouted between **Place Pigalle** and **Place Clichy**, joined by a profusion of taverns and brothels. At certain hours of the day, vapors of alcohol condensed like clouds over the area. One can glimpse something of the Montmartre that was, in the paintings of Toulouse-Lautrec, the great portrayer of nightlife, dancers, drunkards and streetwalkers.

MONTMARTRE

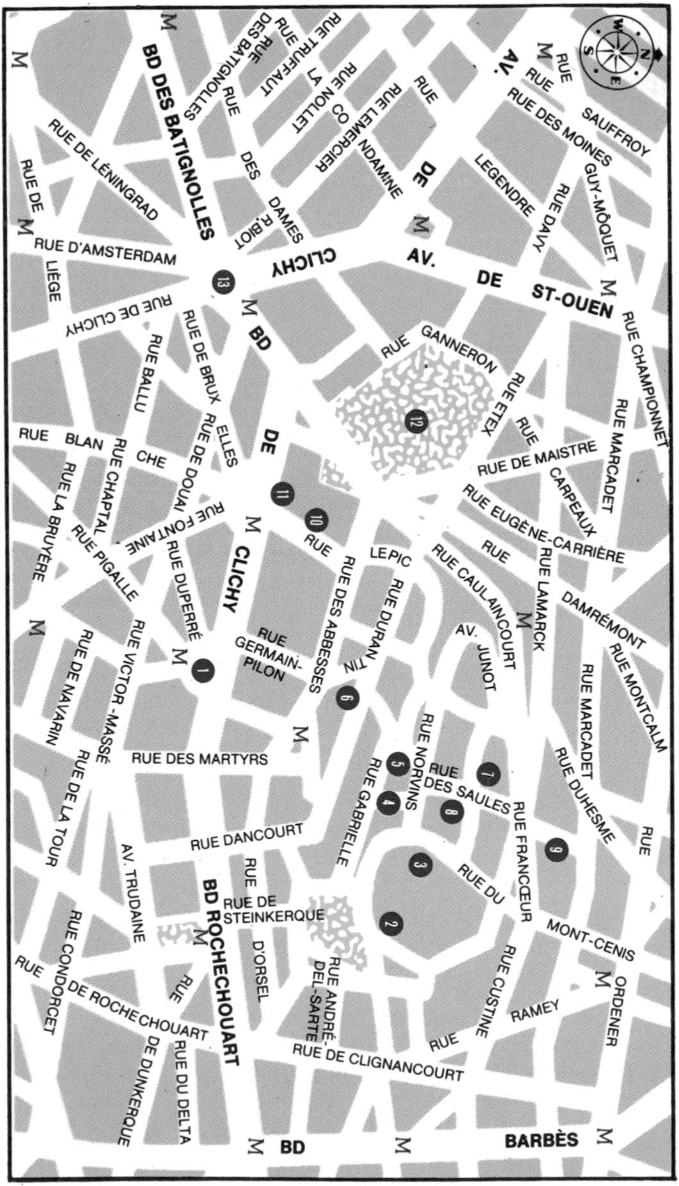
BD DES BATIGNOLLES
RUE DES BATIGNOLLES
RUE TRUFFAUT
RUE LA CONDAMINE
RUE NOLLET
RUE LEMERCIER
RUE DES DAMES
R. BIOT
RUE DE
RUE SAUFFROY
RUE DES MOINES
GUY-MÔQUET
LEGENDRE
RUE DAVY
RUE DE LÉNINGRAD
RUE DE LIÈGE
RUE D'AMSTERDAM
AV. DE CLICHY
AV. DE ST-OUEN
RUE DE CLICHY
RUE BALLU
RUE DE BRUXELLES
BD DE CLICHY
RUE GANNERON
RUE ETEX
RUE CHAMPIONNET
RUE MARCADET
RUE BLANCHE
RUE DE MAISTRE
RUE CARPEAUX
RUE EUGÈNE-CARRIÈRE
RUE LA BRUYÈRE
RUE CHAPTAL
RUE DE DOUAI
RUE FONTAINE
RUE PIGALLE
RUE DUPERRÉ
RUE LEPIC
RUE DES ABBESSES
RUE DURANTIN
RUE CAULAINCOURT
RUE LAMARCK
RUE DAMRÉMONT
RUE MONTCALM
AV. JUNOT
RUE GERMAIN-PILON
RUE DE NAVARIN
RUE VICTOR-MASSÉ
RUE DES MARTYRS
RUE NORVINS
RUE DES SAULES
RUE GABRIELLE
RUE FRANCŒUR
RUE DUHESME
RUE DE LA TOUR
RUE DANCOURT
AV. TRUDAINE
RUE DE STEINKERQUE
BD ROCHECHOUART
RUE D'ORSEL
RUE DU MONT-CENIS
RUE CONDORCET
RUE DE ROCHECHOUART
RUE ANDRÉ-DEL-SARTE
RUE CUSTINE
RUE RAMEY
RUE ORDENER
RUE DE DUNKERQUE
RUE DU DELTA
RUE DE CLIGNANCOURT
BD BARBÈS
M
1
2
3
4
5
6
7
8
9
10
11
12
13
N
S
E
W

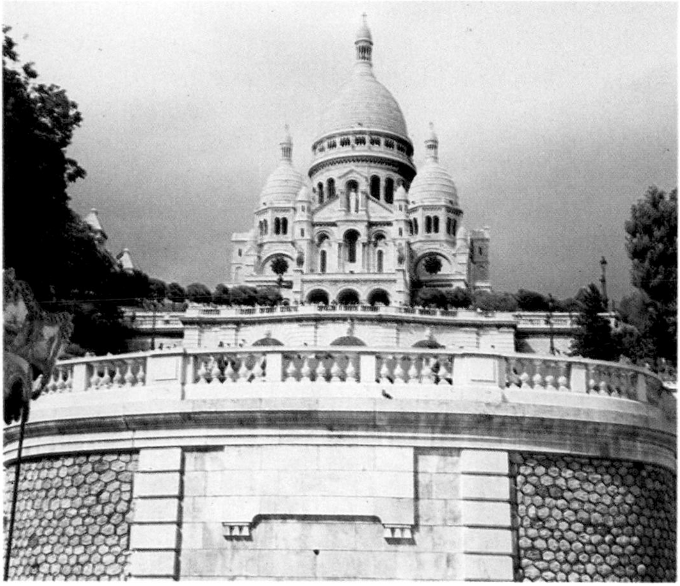

Sacré-Cœur

The decline of Montmartre set in during the 1920s. Around that time, the artists, the heroes of its atmosphere and charm, discovered the Montparnasse area of the left bank and migrated there, "deserting" Montmartre.

Today, though Montmartre is trying to cling by force to the remnants of its past, the authenticity is gone. All that remains is a facade for tourists. Here and there, along the alleyways on the hill and in Musée Montmartre, one can discern shreds of a charm long gone. The nightlife and entertainment district too, is not what it was. The area between Pigalle and Clichy

Index
1. Place Pigalle
2. Basilique du Sacré-Cœur
3. St-Pierre de Montmartre
4. Place du Tertre
5. Musée historique de Montmartre
6. Place Emile Goudeau
7. Cimetière St-Vincent (St-Vincent Cemetery)
8. Musée Montmartre
9. Musée d'art juif
10. Rue Lepic
11. Moulin Rouge
12. Montmartre cemetery
13. Place de Clichy

hosts a great concentration of sex shops, porn cinemas and cheap strip shows.

By metro, get off at Place Clichy, Blanche, Pigalle, Anvers, Abbesses or (on the north side of the hill) Lamarck-Caulaincourt. By bus, lines 30, 54, 67, 80, or 95.

The tour begins at the exit of the Anvers metro station. Head north up rue de Steinkerque to the base of the hill. Look up for a glimpse of **Basilica Sacré-Cœur** (Holy Heart). To reach it, take the steps up the landscaped slope, or use the small cablecar (Fr. *funiculaire*).

The plaza in front of the church opens onto the city to the south and on clear days one can see for miles and miles. The view to the north is just as good. The white church's position is so prominent that it is seen from many places in and out of Paris.

Sacré-Cœur was established in the wake of an idea germinated by the mood of nationalism and hope during the harsh Franco-Prussian War of 1870. Construction got underway five years later, but the work was interrupted at length. It was completed in 1914, just at the start of the next war, World War I. After another delay, the church opened officially in 1919. For many French it became the focus of religious and patriotic identification. This aura came to the fore during the Nazi occupation as well. The Basilica was open around the clock and silent protest vigils stood watch until the occupation ended.

Inside is one of the world's largest mosaics, a depiction of Jesus and the Apostles. A staircase at the left of the interior hall leads to the soaring dome.

West of the basilica stands a monastery dating from the Middle Ages — **St.-Pierre-de-Montmartre**, an architectural integration of a Roman base and a Gothic arcade, which dates back to the second half of the 12th century. Past the monastery is **Place du Tertre**. The square and its attendant cafes are usually packed with tourists, two-penny instant-portrait artists, and paper-etchers who, with a swipe of the scissors, produce your profile. Other "artists" sell "original" Montmartre landscapes to a never-ending stream of enthusiastic clients. Some consider this an amusing sight, but it is really nothing but a distant and commercialized echo of the Montmartre of yesteryear.

Just off the northwestern corner of the square is **Musée Historique de Montmartre**, 11 rue Poulboat, 18e, tel. 46.06.78.92. Open during the summer, daily 10:30am-12:30pm, 2:30-5:30pm. From Nov.-April the museum is only open Wed., Sat. and Sunday and on holidays. Admission fee.

This entertaining museum portrays scenes from the history of Montmartre and Paris in sets and wax figures, ranging from Henry IV to Toulouse-Lautrec. It's definitely a pleasant way to imbibe traces of the past and an opportunity to become an invisible onlooker in the rooms where the events took place.

From the plaza, stroll west through the picturesque little lanes, Ravignan and Norvins, which lead you to **Place Emile-Goudeau**, a plaza with a village atmosphere, which used to be typical of the old Montmartre. Here is where, at the turn of the century, in flimsy wooden structures, many artists started out their artistic lives. Picasso lived here, and this is where he painted his famous work *The Ladies from Avignon* which is said to be the beginning of cubism. Among others, Modigliani and Max Jacob also painted here. Until recently, one could still see these shacks, but a fire which broke out in 1970 completely incinerated them.

Several of the prominent figures from that period and others can be found not far from here in **Cimetière St. Vincent**, several hundred meters to the north. Near the cemetery too, is Montmartre's remaining vineyard. Its grapes still produce wine each year and the harvest is celebrated on the first Saturday of October.

Next to the vineyard is another museum, housed in one of the oldest buildings in the area: **Musée de Montmartre**, 17 rue St. Vincent, 18e, tel. 46.06.61.11. Open daily 2:30-5:30pm, Sun. from 11am, closed Mon. Admission fee.

Renoir, Van Gogh, Utrillo, Dufy and many other artists are said to have resided here for various periods as tenants or guests. The museum is devoted to them and to the French statesman Clémenceau, who was once Mayor of Montmartre.

A third museum in Montmartre, to the north of the little St. Vincent cemetery, is **Musée d'Art Juif** (Museum of Jewish Art), 42 rue des Saulec, 18e, tel. 42.57.84.15. Open weekdays 3-6pm, closed Sat.-Sun., Jewish holidays and August. Admission fee.

The museum (est. 1949), on the third floor of the Montmartre Jewish Center, houses collections of religious artifacts, Jerusalem miniatures, ancient books, sculpture, etchings and paintings, folk art from Western Europe and North Africa and more.

After exploring the alleys of the western section, come down from the hill via rue Lepic. The artist Van Gogh lived for many years at no. 54. At the bottom, the street turns into a flourishing fruit, vegetable, meat and seafood market. The descent ends at **Place Blanche**, home of the famous *Moulin Rouge* nightclub. Its rooftop windmill hints at *Quartier* Montmartre's past.

Head west from the square on Blvd. de Clichy. A right turn onto Avenue Rachel leads to the large **cemetery of Montmartre**. Located here are the burial plots of nobility, and the tombstones of famous individuals such as Degas, Stendhal, Berlioz and Alexandre Dumas Jr., the Goncourt brothers of literary fame (whose name graces France's most important literary prize), and Madame Recamier, the society matron who lent her name to the famous Recamier sofa. The last personality of importance to be buried in this cemetery is movie director François Truffaut.

On leaving the cemetery, on the same road, continue right on the boulevard, which makes a sharp left turn, bringing you to **Place de Clichy**. In the past, this was a popular spot with the bohemian crows, pub crawlers and prostitutes. The character of the area earned immortalization in Henry Miller's novel *Tranquil Days in Clichy*, which is set in the 1920s. On the square there is also a restaurant-cafe, *Wepler*, a very popular spot with Miller. Today, too, it is extremely pleasant to sit here and enjoy a good meal. Their oyster platter has made a name for itself throughout Paris. For those who prefer something less fancy, the country-style chicken is recommended. Price for a meal could be about 250f, while the set-menu costs 140f.

Paris rooftops

Flea Markets, Malls and Antique Dealers

Why are flea markets called flea markets? A fifth generation trader in old artifacts who presently hawks walking sticks, pipes and old lighters in one of these markets, offered an explanation (one of many) which has been passed from generaton to generation. At one time during the winter, the gloomy, mold-infested houses allowed fleas to infest bedding, furniture, clothes, etc. When dry weather returned, people would take their belongings outside, dry them out and shake away the fleas. Passersby would make bids on the objects and deals were actually transacted at times. Hence "flea markets"...

The less formal these markets are, the more volatile they become. One can trust them only so far. Things change swiftly there — from week to week, from visit to visit. "Bargain of the century" stories abound: someone picked up an old painting, engraving, antique, etc. for next-to-nothing, and it proved later to be a long-forgotten masterpiece which its finder sold for millions. Though this has happened, the foreign tourist has a negligible chance of pulling it off. The dealers would not let a work of art or a valuable antique pass their stalls unappraised. Ordinary bargain-hunting, by contrast, is much in vogue here. Counterfeits are rife (especially of furnishings and art), so be careful not to get fooled. Before committing yourself to an expensive purchase, consult with an objective connoisseur.

Most of these markets operate only several days a week (details below). As a rule, it is best to get there as early as possible on the first day of their weekly activity, or in the afternoon of the last day. Insiders say these are the best times for good deals. There are two kinds of merchants here: operators of registered stalls in fixed locations, who pay the market management for the privilege, and "moonlighters", who spread their goods on the ground on the market edges, their ears and eyes ever alert to the approach of inspectors. For those who enjoy haggling, the moonlighters are easier marks.

PARIS

A list of Paris' flea markets follows:

Les Puces de St.-Quen, or **les Puces de Clignancourt**, two names for one market at the edge of town, on the outskirts of *Quartier 18.* From Porte de Clignancourt metro station and walk about 200 yards (200 m) north. Open Sat., Sun. and Mon., from morning until sunset. This is Paris' largest flea market, with hundreds of shops and stalls. It is also the oldest, most formal and least interesting in terms of bargains. Because its tough inspectors keep most amateur dealers off the grounds, the field is left to the professionals whose prices are generally high. One exception is clothing, and inexpensive and occasionally superb merchandise is available. Manufacturers' labels are removed, as are one or two zeroes off the price.

Those with military taste in clothing, can find anything they want in "U.S. Army Surplus" line. Today these items are actually manufactured by civilian companies, but they still look right.

Les **Puces de Montreuil**, Paris' second-largest flea market is becoming "institutionalized", like les Puces de Clignancourt. Something of the genuine flea market spirit survives here just the same. This market too is at the edge of town, on the outskirts of *Quartier 20.* Porte de Montreuil metro station. Les Puces de Montreuil, too, is active Sat., Sun. and Mon., mainly in the morning.

Moonlighters abound on the fringes of this market. One may even encounter some real junkhogs who vend sundry items while scouring the streets of Paris — from bent nails and used toothbrushes to abandoned cars. These "merchants" rarely have anything of real value to offer but they certainly lend an interesting hue to the general scene. Inside the marketplace, are the regular display stalls. Look for interesting old records, yellowed books and manuscripts, *fin de siècle* household goods and the bric-à-brac which serves as the foundation of flea markets everywhere. The determining factor is luck.

The Montreuil flea market is more pleasant than its big brother in Clignancourt. It still offers an occasional adventure in commerce, and exudes a spirit of gaiety and *joie de vivre.*

Les Puces d'Aligre is a downscale but charming market which has proven favorable to those with luck and an ear to the ground. It is located in *Quartier 12* at Place d'Aligre. From Ledru-Rollin metro station turn east on rue Faubourg St.-Antoine and right on rue d'Aligre. Open every morning except Monday.

Peddlars gather and spread out their goods, some on counters and others on the sidewalk flagstones, next to a bustling fruit and vegetable market in the small plaza. The spirit of yesteryear reigns, and the offerings include some real beauties, sometimes at ridiculous prices. An example of the author's own experience from a few years back is a gorgeous set of 6 green-tinted liqueur glasses for 1f apiece! Your luck may be no worse. Highly recommended.

Les Puces de Vanves, a less famous flea market, is also at the edge of town. Porte de Vanves metro station. The market spreads out along av. March Sangier, and spills onto rue Georges-Lafenestre, which it crosses. Here, again, the visitor encounters a blend, less rich, of transient peddlers and regualr merchants. Open Sat. and Sun.

Marché Saint-Germain, located next to 3 rue Mabillon. Mabillon metro station. A small but colorful market, which focuses almost exclusively on old postcards. A real experience for collectors. Open every Wednesday, 9am-1pm, and 4-6:60pm.

Marché du Livre Ancien et d'Occasion, the market for antique and bargain books, is located on rue Brancion, next to Parc Georges Brassens. Open Sat. and Sun from 9am till nightfall.

Malls

We have chosen to mention certain malls in this section because of their special character, their atmosphere of bygone days and for the many shops, selling wonderful "nonsense" which line them. The malls, or *les passages* as the are called, are a memento from the end of the 18th and turn of the 19th centuries. These are narrow little lanes running between the buildings, all in different styles — neo-classical, Art Nouveau, etc. The sun's rays penetrate the glass ceilings over the malls, making a visit to the *passages* a delightful experience, even if you don't intend to shop. Here is a list of a few, which are worth a visit if you are in neighborhood:

Passage du Caire: 2, Place du Caire, Sentier metro station.

Passage des Pavillon: 6, rue de Beaujolais, Pyramides metro station.
Galerie Véro-Dodat: 19, rue J.J. Rousseau, Louvre metro station.
Passage des Princes: 97, rue de Richelieu, Richelieu-Drouot metro station.
Passage Choiseul: 23, rue St.-Augustin, 4-Septembre metro station.
Passage Jouffroy: 12, bd. Montmartre, Richelieu-Drouot metro station.
Galerie Vivienne: 4, rue des Petits-Champs, Bourse metro station.
Passage des Panoramas: 11, bd. Montmartre, rue Montmartre metro station.

New Antique Dealers

Over the past few years, several of Paris' antique dealers felt a need to gather together in new centers which were either built or renovated for this purpose. Consequently, a number of large complexes have come about, which allow the tourist access to hunderds of antique shops within one area. Here he can see and buy a variety of antique pieces from different periods. Generally, the prices are fair, and its almost impossible to find bargains. Nevertheless, this concentration of shops creates a special atmosphere — turning it into a sort of vibrant museum.

These are a few antique dealers centers:

Le Louvre des Antiquités: 2, Place Palais-Royal, Palais-Royal metro station, near the Louvre. Over 250 shops selling antiques, which offer a huge range of art works form different periods, furniture, utensils, etc. Open every day 11am-7pm. Closed Monday.

Le Village Suisse: 78, av. de Suffren, La Motte-Picquet-Grenelle metro station. Dozens of shops selling antiques, furniture, bric-à+brac, etc. Open daily 10:30am-7pm. Closed Tues. and Wed.

La Cour Aux Antiquaires: 54, rue du Faubourg St.-Honoré, Concorde metro station. Antique, antiques and more antiques for lots of new money! Open daily 10:30am-6:30pm. Closed Sunday and Monday.

Bit of Country in the Middle of Town

As crowded as Paris has become from one generation to the next, the city has nevertheless discovered the secret of preserving patches of greenery, charming parks between its neighborhoods, and, above all, two real forests — Bois (Forest) de Boulogne to the west, and Bois de Vincennes to the east. Paris' 330 parks cover a total area of approx. 40 sq/km. Some bear names which reflect Parisian history, some are repositories of art (especially scuplture), and others are works of art in their own right.

Bois de Boulogne

This charming park covers 8.5 sq/km, and abounds with little playgrounds, sports facilities, artificial lakes and more than 140,000 trees. Bois de Boulogne began as a royal hunting ground which the various kings loved mainly for its proximity to Paris. It was "renovated" under Napoléon III: about 25 miles (40 km) of paths were paved, and lakes and reservoirs dug. For many generatons, Boulogne was the place "to see and be seen". The rich and the noble crisscrossed the park on foot, horsback or coach, showing off the best of their wardrobes. Today, bus 244, departing from a station in Porte Maillot, plies the park's roads and links its many attractions.

One of these attractions is **La Bagatelle**, open daily 8:30am-7:30pm. The garden was laid out in 1778 for the Count of Artois, a little boy who was to be crowned Charles X. Visit the castle, some artificial caves, romantic archeological "relics" and dancing waterfalls. Today la Bagatelle also has an amusement park — **Jardin d'Acclimatation** — with a train, children's games, a hall of mirrors, a doll museum, a zoo, an exhibit of old-style shops, and much more. To come here directly, Sablons metro station. Open 10am-6pm. Admission fee, and the various attractions can be quite costly for each little person...

Jardin Shakespeare is located in the part of Bois de Boulogne known as **Pré Catelan**. It boasts an amphitheater and a stage with a natural "set". Actors step on and off stage between rocks, bushes and trees; all around are species of plant life which the great English bard mentioned in his dramas. Guided tours 11am, 3pm and 5pm. Admission fee.

One of the finest ways to explore Boulogne is by bicycle. Rent one at **Pavillon Royal**; get off the bus at the large lake and ask for directions.

Bois de Vincennes

Paris' second forest is larger than Boulogne but has always been less fashionable (for no discernible reason). East of Porte Dorée metro station. By bus (which in this case is more convenient), take line 46 or 86.

Bois de Vincennes, too, served as a royal hunting ground until it was presented to the people as a public park by Louis XV. Its 4 sq/miles (10 sq/km) harbor some 130,000 trees, 9 stadiums for various sports, riding paths, lakes, restaurants, play facilities, etc.

Vincennes is also home of the **Great Zoological Garden of Paris** (est. 1934). Open daily 9am-6pm, 6:30pm on Sun. (in winter till 5:30pm). Admission fee. The zoo shelters more than 1,100 animals (including extremely rare species such as the panda, which gave birth in 1985). The management takes great pains to construct "natural" mini-habitats for the animals. This, of course, makes the zoo a more interesting place to visit.

Le Parc Floral de Paris, Paris' flower garden, is also situated in Bois de Vincennes, near the Château. Château de Vincennes metro station. Open daily 9:30am-5pm, summers till 6pm. Admission fee, children to age 6 free. The park, a must for flower lovers, bursts with tens of thousands of species, colors and sizes. A cute little train winds through the park daily during the summer, and on Sat. and Sun. during the rest of the year. A fare is charged for the train ride. Recommended.

A **Buddhist Center** with a massive sculptured Buddha, a relic of an international exposition held here on 1931, can also be visited at Bois de Vincennes.

Parc Montsouris

This is one of the most charming parks in Paris. By metro, take the RER line from Denfert-Rochereau to Cité Universitaire. By bus, take the PC, which plies a "circle route" passing the gates of Paris.

In Montsouris, established at the end of the reign of Napoléon III, is a replica of the palace of the Bey (Sultan) of Tunisia. It was presented to the city of Paris for an exposition held there in 1867. Though it has been abandoned and neglected in recent years, a renovation plan is in progress. The park also includes an artificial lake and Paris' weather station.

Parc Monceau

Enter this romantic, graceful and imaginative park through gates embellished with gilded metal reliefs. Designed in the late 18th century for the Duke of Orléans, the park offers an entertaining eclectic of classical-style columns with a Roman ruin look, chestnut trees and rich greenery. Monceau metro station, or bus 30, 84 or 94.

Parc Georges Brassens

This is the largest park established in Paris in recent years (namely, since Napoléon III). Named for the beloved French singer Georges Brassens, who died several years ago, it was set up on the site of the former Paris abattoir. Where one used ot hear the bellowing of cattle facing the slaughterer's knife, the visitor now hears the gurgling of an artificial river and the laughter of children busy at play or enjoying one of the frequent puppet shows. Convention metro station or bus 39 or 49.

Jardin des Plantes (Botanical Gardens)

Louis XIII's garden of medicinal herbs has evolved into a vast botanical garden which includes a nature museum and a modest zoo, believed to be the oldest in France. Open 9am-5pm; museum closed Tues. Gare d'Austerlitz, Jussieu, or Place Monge metro stations, bus 61, 65, 67, or 91.

Jardin Alber-Kahn

Located between rue des Abondances and Quai du 4-Septembre in Boulogne. Pont de St.-Cloud metro station. Buses 52 and 72. Even those who are usually indifferent to gardens, will probably be enthusiastic about this special corner of greenery. It is the personal creation of an extremely wealthy diamantaire of Jewish extraction, who lived in the late 19th century. This park was the fulfillment of his wild

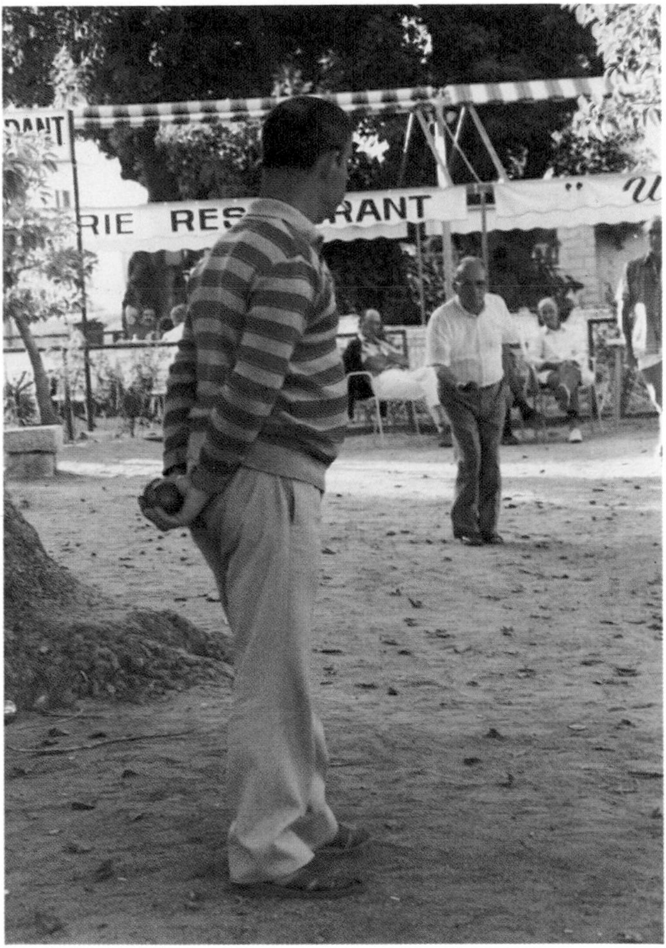

Games in the Park

dream, namely to create a garden containing the different scenery he had seen on his travels.

The dream was realized and the result is wonderous: a Japanese garden, an English garden, a French garden, something of the northern forests, a rock garden and much more. In spring, when the flowers are in bloom, it is a breathtaking experience. The gardens are open daily 9:30am-12:30pm and 2-6pm.

Versailles — Paris' Summer Home

An explorer in Paris, city of the French Revolution, must not overlook Versailles, about 15 miles (25km) southwest of Paris. Apart from the extraordinary beauty and grandeur of this city, a visit to Versailles undoubtely provides some of the most convincing clues available to the special historical background leading to the revolution. The Château of Versailles was converted by Louis XIV into his residence and seat of government. Versailles, now as then, symbolises the absolute monarchy, and as such was a source of great provocation to the Third Estate.

The city of Versailles itself was founded in the 17th century and today has a population of nearly 100,000. The most convenient way of getting there from Paris is by train: Montparnasse, or Saint-Lazare stations. By RER, take the C5 line east. By bus, take No. 171, which leaves from next to the Pont de Sévres metro station. By car, take highway N10, which leaves Paris via Porte de St-Cloud, in the southwestern part of town.

Le Château de Versailles: Located in the western section of Versailles, the Château had a modest infancy as a hunting hostel of the French royal family. Under Louis XIII it grew into a summer home and under Louis XIV, into the opulent, massive palace seen today. More than 30,000 laborers and some 6,000 horses toiled for nearly 20 years to produce the Château and its embellishment, gardens and water pools.

The King with his court, an entourage of more than 1,000 noblemen, army commanders and senior officials moved to Versailles in 1682. During the reign of Louis XV, the palace was somewhat neglected, and the court returned to Paris. However, this was a short-lived move, because as mentioned the big crowded city was not suited to the comforts of the monarchy. With the coronation of Louis XVI, Versailles was reinstated as the royal center.

This court, from its seat in Versailles, imposed absolute rule over France until it was driven from power and out of the palace during the Revolution. It was in October of 1789, that Louis XVI and Marie-Antoinette succumbed to the angry crowd and left the palace forever.

In 1793, the revolutionary National Convention, which controlled France and which later declared the First Republic, decided to have a general clearance sale of all the palace treasures. Thousands of *objets d'art,* suites of furniture, art works and much more, found their way to merchants and from there were dispersed among the wealthy in France and the rest of the world. It was the decision of Louis-Philippe who reigned 1830-1848, to turn Versailles into a historical museum. The palace was renovated, and a collection of valuables appropriate to the grandeur of the place, including some originals, were brought to replace what had been sold.

From the train station, cross Place d'Armes parade ground. The Château plaza is entered through a set of iron gates next to one of the royal stables. Note the statue of Louis XIV. The steps at the western end of the plaza lead to the palace chapel. While inside, notice the white and gold ceiling, a masterful, illustrated display of grandeur.

A fixed, well-designed route leads through the **Grand Appartement** of the Château and to the renowned **Hall of Mirrors**, whose mirrors reflect the garden landscape outside. The famous Treaty of Versailles, which officially brought World War I to an end, was signed here in 1919. Even visitors who are not moved by the historical events will no doubt be overwhelmed at the sight of the magnificent hall — 240 ft. (73 m) long, approx. 30 ft. (10 m) wide, 42 ft. (13 m) high, with 17 vaulted windows all around.

The next stop is the **King's Suite** and the royal bedroom. The royal court would assemble here every morning and evening to observe the rising and retiring ceremonies of the King of France, the most eventful moments on the royal schedule. Louis XIV died in this bed in September 1715. The ornate balustrade is a more recent addition, it was installed to save the bed from the hands of visitors.

The tour proceeds to the **Queen's Suite** and the **Coronation Hall**. The regal couple had additional quarters in the southern wing. These were for amusements of a decidedly private nature, which have never found their way into royal history.

Versailles — grandeur without and within

The Royal Opera occupies a highly impressive structure at the edge of the northern wing, built entirely of carved wood embellished in blue, pink and gold. This masterpiece, built under Louis XV, staged special performances for the royal couple and their court, including one-time shows, preceded by numerous rehearsals and substantial outlay.

Les Jardins de Versailles: The wonderful Château gardens spread out to the west of the palace. Here the royal court enjoyed its outings and sought its amusement in the open air. Ornate terraces, flowerbeds carefully pruned in classical French-style, statues, fountains (Apollo is the largest and most impressive), a large cross-shaped canal with an axis over a mile long on which gondolas and boats cruise — all designed by the great 17-century landscape architect Le Nôtre.

Two hostels in the northern section of the garden still serve their intended purpuse for visiting VIPs. **Le Grand Trianon** was built in 1687 under Louis XIV and **Le Petit Trianon** was established in 1755 during Louis XV's reign. Architecturally, both are remarkably beautiful.

Next to these is **Le Hameau**, a miniature village of peasants' huts, a barn, a corral and other farm appurtenances — suitable equipment for the "nature amusement" of the Queen and her maids.

There are different visiting hours for the various sections of the palace. The Kings Suites, the Hall of Mirrors and the Queen's Suite are open daily 9:45am-5pm. Closed Monday.

Le Grand Trianon is open daily 9:45pm-noon and 2-5pm. Closed Monday. Le Petit Trianon is open daily 2-5pm. Closed Monday, and sometimes Sat. and Sun. Entrance fee for the palace and the gardens. An additional fee for Le Grand and Le Petit Trianon. You can either pay for them separately, or purchase a combined ticket for both.

Information on guided tours (in French and English), tel. 39.50.38.32. Information on multimedia shows (sound-and-light, waterplay and dancing fountains) in the palace garden, tel. 39.50.36.52.

The city of Versailles itself, established in the 17th century, exudes the charm of the "golden age" of Louis XIV with its lovely streets, prolific sculptures and impressive plazas, of which **Place Hoche** is the most beautiful. Two churches here are worth visiting: **Notre-Dame** constructed in 1680 and **Saint-Louis** dating from the mid-18th century.

If you are planning to spend the night, the following hotels are recommended:

Trianon Palace: 1, bd. de la Reine, tel. 39.50.34.12; 4-star de luxe, 130 rooms with toilet, bath and color TV, view of Jardins de Versailles.
Bellevue Hôtel: 12 av. de Sceaux, tel. 39.50.13.41; 3-star, 24 rooms.
Le Versailles: 7, rue Sainte-Anne-Petite Place, tel. 39-50-64-65; 3-star, 48 rooms.
Cluny: 6 Imp. de Cluny, tel. 39.50.18.09; 2-star, 20 rooms.

The Other Route — This too Is Paris

The tours in this guide cover most of the city, but, of course, in a city of this scope there are lots of other sites which may be of interest to you, depending on personal taste. This list is intended to give you the option of choosing among the museums and sights. Most of these fall outside the usual scope of interest of tourists in Paris, but some may prove to be exactly what you are looking for.

La Villette

A new complex — which is one of the largest construction projects of the 1980s. Spreading over 90 acres, it includes various institutions, a science and industry museum and much more.

It is best to approach from the northern end of the complex, the entrance of which is at 30, av. Corentin Cariou. Porte de la Villette metro station. Buses 150, 152, 250A and PC. The major attraction of La Villette is the Complex of Science and Industry, **La Cité des Sciences et de L'Industrie**. Open Tues., Thurs. and Fri. 10am-6pm; Wed. noon-9pm. Sat. and Sun. noon-8pm. Entrance fee.

Is it a museum or an unusual "playground"? In fact, it is a little of both. When the facility opened in 1986 it attracted many youngsters and the young at heart, who wanted to gain real knowledge about the world in which we live today: a world of advanced sciences which are incorporated in industry and which influence every part of our daily lives. The impressive modern building, a combination of concrete, steel and glass, has a total area of about 1670 sq. ft. (150 sq/m), of which 335 sq. ft. (30 sq/m) are devoted to the permanent exhibition.

The expansive entrance level is always vibrant and buzzing with throngs of visitors. Here the ticket booths, information counters, a moneychanging bank, souvenir shops, etc. are located. Looking up, it will remind you of the Pompidou Center: a huge modern factory. For those who are interested, on the right hand side of the lobby are video guides which provide information about the various activities available to visitors. Press the screen for the information you require, (also available in English). Escalators take you all the way up to the two exhibition floors.

The number of things to see and do in this center are so numerous that it would be impossible to describe them all. In brief, there are dozens of displays encompassing various topics such as: energy, sound, space, weather, ocean depths, materials, agriculture, light, development of the robot, biology and many more. Unlike the general "do not touch" rule in museums, here the approach is quite different, and everyone is encouraged to press buttons, operate devices, experiment and learn. For example, in "The Forest Theater", press a button and birds start twittering while little puppets demonstrate the work of the forest protectors, and the variety of trees in different areas. In the world of agriculture you can operate sowing, planting and harvesting machinery inside large glass boxes.

The robot corner surveys primitive man's first elephant traps, through the wooden puppet Pinoccio, right up to modern industrial robots. For those of you who have always dreamt about space, here you have the opportunity of entering the control room of a spaceship, which is surrounded by moving screens which simulate the sensation of flight. You can also put on a spacesuit and step out of the spaceship.

In other areas, changing exhibitions are mounted on different topics and there are special halls for international congresses and symposiums. Children between the ages of 3-12 are invited to test their ability through scientific games in the "Discoveries" section.

Behind the museum is a round shiny metal structure known as **La Geode**, which should not be missed on a visit to La Villette. This 120 ft (36m) sphere is coated with mirror-like stainless steel in which the surroundings are reflected. Inside, there is seating for 370 spectators who have the opportunity of seeing the world's largest sceen. This 11,000 sq. ft. (1,000 sq/m) convex screen is used for the screening of 180 degree films, with highly sophisticated acoustics. The program consists mostly of nature films, deep-sea dives, voyages into space, etc. The effect is unparalleled and the audience feels like it is inside the films. This is an experience which has to be seen to be believed, There are daily screenings between 10am-6pm, every hour on the hour. On the weekends, they continue until 9pm. For details or bookings, call tel. 40.05.06.07 or 46.42.13.13.

Also within the La Villette complex is **Le Zénith**, a super-modern concert hall, which can accommodate an audience of 6,400 for the pop-rock concerts which are staged here. On the other side of the complex, next to the Porte de Pantin metro station, is the elongated building of **La Grande Halle**, the big market. It was built in the 19th century as a livestock market, but has now undergone extensive renovations which fortunately did not spoil the charm of the period architecture. Today it serves as a venue for large-scale exhibitions, fairs, congresses, etc.

And this is not all. The complex also has other lovely areas of lawns and rich greenery, an exciting amusement park for children, a pleasant coffee shop, and more.

L'Institut du Monde Arabe

This Institute of the Arab World is located at 23, Quai St.-Bernard, tel. 46.43.25.25. Cardinal-Lemoine metro station. Open daily 1-8pm. Closed Monday. Entrance fee.

In the 1980s, an impressive building was constructed near the Seine, opposite the eastern end of Ile St.-Louis, to serve as venue for an encounter with the Islamic culture. The architect Jean Nobel used modern materials — glass and aluminium with marble, but the final result is a juxtaposition of modernity with traditional motifs of Arabic architecture; minarets, courtyards, arches, fountains and the use of shadow and light in Oriental style.

This institute serves as a center for researchers, students and visitors who wish to witness the richness of Islamic art and culture. At their disposal is a large library of Arab writings, historical documents, and a permanent exhibition as well as changing exhibits on different topics. On the ninth floor of the institute, you can also taste delicacies from the Islamic kitchen in all its varieties. The restaurant serves, among other things, *kabab* and sweet *baklava* (pistachio filled pastry dripping in honey).

Musée de la Publicité

Museum of Advertising, 18, rue Paradis, tel. 42.46.13.09.

Château-d'Eau metro station. Open daily noon-6pm. Closed Tuesday. Entrance fee.

This attractive building, which used to house a well-known ceramics warehouse, today serves as the venue for a fascinating museum. The museum is a must, especially for anyone who is involved in advertising. The treasures of this establishment include advertising posters and notices from the 18th century until today. Because of the huge amount of material available, the exhibits are displayed in rotation and are changed regularly. There are also exhibits showing advertising through different media — radio, television, newspapers, film and video. Changing exhibits reveal unusual and special aspects of the field. For example, one dealt with the role of great artists, painters and others in the advertising business.

Musée Marmottan

Located at 2, Louis-Boilly, tel. 42.24.07.02. La Muette metro station. Open 10am-5:30pm. Closed Monday. Entrance fee.

This museum stands on the western edge of the city, where it merges with Bois de Boulogne. In recent years, the museum was rescued from obscurity, and suddenly became popular. During the 19th century, this was the home of the historian Paul Marmottan, and his brother Jules, the art collector. The museum, which was established after their deaths, houses a collection of furniture, works of art, and *objets d'art* from different periods, in particular from the Rennaisance and the Napoleonic era. The finest pieces of the collection used to be two wonderful wall carpets, work of the Flemish school, but their glory has been eclipsed by a collection of Impressionist paintings which was presented to the museum. An absolute treat for art lovers.

Among the artists represented are works by Monet, Renoir, Pissarro, Sisley, Gauguin and others. The museum made the headlines in 1985, when thieves broke in and made off with Monet's *Impression: Sunrise.*

There has been no trace of either the paintings or the perpetrators of the theft.

Musée d'Art Naïf

The Museum of Naive Art is located at 2, rue Ronsard,

tel. 42.58.74.12. Anvers metro station. Open daily 10am-6pm. Entrance fee.

Lovers of this very specific type of art will find here brief respite from the controversy surrounding this art form. On the first floor, there are works on loan from the Max Fornay collection. including drawings, sculptures and aquarelles — which are simultaneously amusing and amazing. The ground floor hosts changing exhibitions, in a new spirit: a creative subject with the participants of visitors. Interesting for children and adults alike.

Musée de Radio-France

116, av. du Président Kennedy, tel. 42.30.21.80. Passy metro station. Guided tours every day at 10:30am, 11:30am. 3:30pm and 4:30pm. Closed Sunday. Entrance fee.

A real gem for radio buffs, this museum surveys the development of the radio, since its invention, through documentation, photographs, varied and strange instruments, among them, those of Marconi himself!

Musée de la Franc-Maçonnerie

The Museum of Freemasons, 12, rue Cadet, tel. 45.23.20.92. Cadet metro station. Open daily 2-6pm. Closed Sunday. Entrance free. Those who are connected with, or curious about, the mystery of the institution of Freemasons, can learn something on a visit to this museum. It is fascinating to view the ceremonial instruments and special clothing. It is also interesting to keep in mind that a number of great men have been members of this order — from the philosopher Voltaire to President Roosevelt.

Paris' peripheral Cities

By virtue of its centrality, in recent centuries, Paris has attracted new residents from all over the country. Paris is geographically compact, and many flourishing communities and population centers have sprouted in the vicinity, some of which have now become cities. Today, Paris is enveloped in two belts of cities — "the nearby suburbs" and "the outer suburbs". Below is a survey of attractive and intriguing places which are worth a visit. The closer cities can generally be reached by metro, while buses from the "city gates" depart for more distant areas. Alternatively, there are the R.E.R. lines or the suburban trains which depart from Paris.

Versailles

This is the city which gave its name to the most famous and most visited royal château in the world. (See "Versailles — Paris' Summer Home"). While most flock only to see the palace, there is also a museum here which is certainly worth visiting for those who have the time. **Musée Lambinet**, 54, bd. de la Reine, tel. 39.50.30.32. Open daily 2-6pm. Closed Monday. Entrance fee. Make a sharp left turn on exiting the palace gates, and then continue along rue des Réservoirs until you reach the boulevard where the museum is located. It is housed in a beautiful palace dating back to the 18th century.

Among the museum's exhibits is a collection of sculptures, the work of Jean Antoine Houdon, who was born in Versailles in 1741 and lived to the ripe old age of 87. He is best known for his portrait sculptures of famous personalities such as Rousseau, Voltaire, Diderot and Franklin. He was greatly praised for the exact likeness of his sculpted heads.

You can also view ancient ceramic utensils, which are extremely lovely, and 18th century furniture. Do not miss out on the beautiful gardens.

Mary-le-Roy

Next to Versailles and set in a stunningly beautiful park, it was the royal lodge where kings and their nobles stayed during their hunting trips in the area. You can visit daily 2-5:30pm. Closed Monday. Entrance fee. Along the Seine, within city limits, is the famous Marly pump. Dating back to 1681, this is an impressive machine and an extraordinary specimen of its time. It drew water from the Seine and delivered it to Versailles, where it filled the fountains and ornamental pools in the castle gardens.

Saint-Germain-en-Laye

The birthplace of Louis XIV, the town, built on terraces, has a magnificent view of the Seine valley, and a lovely Renaissance-style castle of the same name. Today the castle accommodates an interesting and well-appointed museum of prehistory, **Musée des Antiquités Nationales**, Place du Château, tel. 34.51.53.65. Open daily 9:45am-noon and 1:30-5:15pm. Closed Tuesday. Entrance fee. Take the R.E.R. A1 going east or bus 158A which leaves from La Défense. By car, take road RN13.

In the mid-19th century, many archeological finds were discovered around the Elysées fortress which is near the town Elysée-Sainte-Reine. These treasures of prehistoric man greatly aroused the enthusiasm of Napoléon III, who was the current ruler of France, and he established the museum. Today, after having made many acquisitions, it is one of the best museums of its kind in the world. The life of primitive man has been reconstructed superbly by means of his tools, his every day belongings, his jewelry and cave drawings which have survived. The stone-age, bronze-age and iron-age, as well as later periods, also receive excellent and interesting coverage at the museum. Definitely worth the trip out.

Between here and Marly is the home of author Alexandre Dumas, "father" of the *Three Musketeers.*

Sceaux

A park and one of the most beautiful places to visit in the entire Paris area. It was built by the French landscape artist Le Nôtre, on a 500-acre plot next to the castle. In the 18th century, this castle (const. 1670) was the venue for the Duchess du Maine's cultural salon, which was very famous at the time. In 1798, after the Revolution, the park and the castle were bought by one of the "tycoons" of the time, for the then-stupendous sum of 750,000f. He planned to destroy all existing structures and use the grounds as a farm. But in 1856, his son-in-law had the park restored and a new castle built on the site,

The castle now houses a museum, **Musée de l'Ile-de-France**, Château-de-Sceaux, tel. 45.61.06.71. Open daily 2-6pm; Sun. and also 10am-noon. Closed Tuesday. Entrance fee. Take the R.E.R. line B4 going south, or buses 128 or 197, which leave from Porte d'Orléans. Besides the lovely castle, the museum also has an impressive collection of 18th and 19th century paintings and sculpture, *objets d'art*, ornate ceramic bowls, suites of furniture and clothes. It provides an interesting look at the opulence of the daily lives of the French aristocracy in their prime.

Saint-Cloud

This city is known for its famous park and towering bluff. The latter is an exciting place to explore in its own right. Château Saint-Cloud made the history books as the place where Emperor Napoléon and Marie-Louise of Austria were married in a ceremony of grandeur and extraordinary pomp. Fate then took over; the castle was seized several years later by Field Marshall von Blucher of Prussia, and the surrender of Paris was signed here in 1815.

Sèvres

Near Parc Saint-Cloud, it is a major center of France's porcelain industry. The porcelain operation, once a royal industry, was established by Madame de Pompadour, Louis XV's highly influential mistress who loved porcelain. The city also hosts the **Musée de Céramique** (Porcelain Museum of France) and its splendid and rare collections of this art form. Place de la Manufacture, tel. 45.34.99.05. Pont-de-Sèvres metro station. Open 10am-noon and 1:30-5:15pm. Closed Tuesday. Entrance fee.

The variety of objects which have been created in porcelain is astounding: human and animal figures, decorations, flowers, imaginative creations, serving bowls and crockery. At the museum you can see it all, display after display of beautiful porcelain, all of a high standard. There are even a few tidbits of gossip... you can see the tea service of Madame du Barry, the mistress of Louis XV, who was guillotined in 1793, and more.

You can also visit the factory at Sèvres, on the first and third Thursday of every month, from 1-3:30pm. Closed during the summer months.

The city of Sèvres is honored by weighty presence of the **International Ministry of Measurments and Weights** which is located here. For those interested in these subjects, the revered institution is at Pavillon de Breteuil.

Rueil-Malmaison

A small residential city west of Paris, it was built over the former "playground" of the kings of France. Cardinal Richelieu, head of Louis XIII's Council of Ministers and the actual ruler of France at the time, built a grand castle here in the early 17th century. Another castle, which still stands, was bought in 1799 by Joséphine, Napoléon's wife during his tenure as a "mere" general. In 1809, after she and Bonaparte divorced, Joséphine retired to the castle until her death on May 25, 1814. Later, ex-Emperor Napoleon spent five days here before sailing off to exile at Ile Sainte-Hélène.

Knowing this, we can now visit **Château de Malmaison**, at av. du Château, tel. 47.49.20.07. Take line A1 east of the R.E.R. or bus 158A which leaves from La Défense. By car, drive along the RN13. Open daily 10am-noon and 1:30-5pm. Closed Tuesday. Entrance fee.

Saint-Denis

Located north of Paris, it is known for the church and abbey of the same name which dates from the 7th century. Christian tradition identifies this as the burial place of Saint-Denis who reached the site after marching nearly 4 miles (6 km) with his head, which the Romans had decapitated, tucked under his arm. The abbey is considered the oldest and the most important in France. The abbey father, Suger, was the effective ruler of France between 1147 and 1149, when Louis VII set out on the Second Crusade. The monks of Saint-Denis were also the fathers of recorded history in France. Their manuscripts, dating from the 8th century, are primary source material in this discipline.

Various kings of France and their families are buried in

the abbey church (const. 1136-1218), and their sculpted likenesses and death masks are on display. During the Revolution, a mob forced its way into the church, destroying large parts of the building, shattering statues and desecrating the royal tombs. Architect Viollette le Duc restored the site to its former glory in 1815. To reach the site, take the metro to St-Denis-Basilique station. A museum near the abbey exhibits, among other items, many relics of the site's past.

Musée d'Art et d'Histoire Saint-Denis, 22 rue Gabriel Péri, tel. 42.43.05.10. St-Denis Porte de Paris metro station. Open daily 10am-5:30pm, Sun. 2-6:30pm. Closed Tuesday. Entrance fee. A great deal of thought went into the establishing of this charming, well-tended museum, which is housed in structures which, in the 17th century, belonged to a Carmelite monastery. It displays a varied selection of exhibits: archeology and medieval ceramic utensils, the history of St-Denis, the history of the Carmelite monastery, documents of the commune of Paris and more.

Vincennes

West of Paris, the nearby forest of Vincennes served as royal hunting grounds since the 9th century. King Philip Augustus, Louis VII's son, built a famous manor house here of stunning dimensions: 1,050 ft (320 m) long, and 585 ft (178 m) wide. His grandson Louis IX (Saint Louis), built Château de Vincennes in the mid-13th century and, tradition claims, sat in judgment of his people under an oak tree in the palace courtyard.

Vincennes was developed, expanded and fortified by Charles V. A prison was added whose inmates included celebrities such as Marquis de Sade. Today, **Château de Vincennes** houses a pair of museums, one of local history and the other devoted to the annals of World War I. You can visit the palace, its towers, the chapel belonging to it and the museums. Château de Vincennes metro station. Open daily 10am-5:30pm (in winter only until 4:15pm). Entrance fee.

Fontainebleau

Located about 30 miles (50 km) southeast of Paris, a forest of the same name surrounds the city and is considered the loveliest in the Paris area.The droves of artists who have flocked to Fontainebleau over the years — Millet, Corot and Troyon are only a few — commemorated various scenes of the forest on canvas. Future mountain climbers take their first groping ventures up the boulders and pitched cliffs that thrust skyward between the trees.

The royal Castle of Fontainebleau was built c. 1520 by François I, on the site of the original castle which had stood there since the 12th century. Its decorative style, though obviously influenced by Italian and French architecture, created the new Fontainebleau school. The place proved to be one of the most loved homes of several generations of French kings.

The château is famous as the site of Napoléon's first resignation in 1814, when he bade his marshalls farewell in an impressive ceremony. During World War II, the Nazis chose Fontainebleau as their headquarters. The city of Fontainebleau hosts a well-appointed military museum and a noted music conservatory.

The train from Gare de Lyon reaches the city, after which take a bus to the castle. By car, drive along highway A6. Open daily 9:30-12:30pm and 2-5pm. Closed Tuesday. Entrance fee.

If you are interested in the history of wars and different types of arms, then visit the **Musée Napoléon d'Art et d'Histoire Militaire**, at 88, rue St-Honoré. Open daily 2-5:30pm. Closed Sunday and Monday. Entrance fee.

Chantilly

28 miles (45 km) north of Paris, Chantilly is best known for its splendid park, an enchanting forest just out of town, a gorgeous and "touristy" château and, above all, its horses. One can reach Chantilly by train from Gare du Nord, or by car along Road RN16.

Le Château de Chantilly was built in the 10th century by the district governor, the nobleman Rotonde de Senlis. It was expanded and beautified over the centuries by its many owners, including the Count of Amartine, Charles V, Prince de Condé, Queen Hortense and Napoléon. You can visit the palace and **Musée Condé** which is housed within the palace walls. Open daily 10am-6pm. Closed Tuesday. Entrance fee. The museum presents a collection of sculpture, paintings, furniture and *objets d'art* from different periods.

Not far from the castle are the stables of Chantilly which are no less opulent than a royal palace. Today 4,000 steeds practice and compete in the large meadow and the race tracks, attracting thousands of visitors from Paris every Sunday. Not far from here is the **Musée Vivant du Cheval** (The Living Museum of the Horse). Besides horses, one can see equestrian sculptures, films and more. Open daily 2-4:40pm. Sat. and Sun. 10:30am-5:30pm. Entrance fee.

La Défense

Just outside Paris, west of Pont de Neuilly, its name stems from the heroic defensive battle fought here against the Germans in the war of 1870-1871, in which Paris was ultimately conquered. In the 1960s, the fate of the area was determined with the commencement of construction of office blocks, of a size unprecedented in Europe. These buildings are intended to alleviate the shortage of office space in Paris itself. The first to go up was C.N.I.T. (National Center for Industry and Trade), which was designed by three architects blessed with vision: Zarfuss, Camelotte and De Mei. Beneath a concrete dome, truncated on three sides, which covers an area of 1 million sq. ft. (90,000 sq/m), they built a whole world of offices and halls for the annual conventions and fairs which are regularly held here.

La Défense, nicknamed "Little New York" by the Parisians, has since the '60s, remained a huge commercial center. A few statistics, by way of demonstrating the point: The Towers of La Défense have a combined 39 million sq.ft (3.5 million sq/m) of office space. 100,000 workers man these offices, which belong to 800 companies, among them 11 of the 100 biggest companies in the world, and 8 of the 10 largest concerns in France. Among others, the Towers house the *Gas and Electricity Cooperation of France*, the office of *Mobil Oil*, *Fiat* and the *Credit Bank of Lyon*.

The project for the 1980s was that of **La Grande Arche de la Défense**, (with a cost of 3.4 billion francs). From a distance, the 35-floor office block resembles an empty cube. Into this empty space, one could fit, without any difficulty, the entire Notre-Dame Cathedral, including its lofty turrets. The building is coated in white marble, quarried from the Carrara mountains in Italy, the most famous source of sculpting-marble.

The southern "pillar" of the arch belongs to the *Government Ministry for Heavy Industries*, while the northern side is for various national companies. The panoramic viewpoint from the roof of the arch allows the public a view of the near and more distant surroundings. Ascend in any of the 4 panoramic elevators found in the building. The "Arch" is constructed on a single axis which starts at the Louvre, passes through the Concorde Obelisk, continues along the Champs Elysées until it reaches the opening of the Arc de Triomphe. The symbolic significance of this requires no explanation.

There are more plans on the go for the area during the 1990s — a no less daring architectural feat. Plans are for a thin, pipe-like, office block which will tower 1,300 ft (400m) high. It will be constructed of glass and steel, and the color will gradually get lighter the higher it goes. The architect behind this vision is Jean Nobel who designed the Institute of the Arab World.

The commercial center, **Quatre Temps**, includes hotels, restaurants, cinemas, game arcades, an ice-skating rink and a broad spectrum of shops. To reach all this opulence, take the R.E.R. to La Défense station or bus 73. Within a few years, the metro line, which currently ends at Pont de Neuilly, will be extended to reach the area.

"Musts"

Visitors with a few days to spend in Paris will probably confront the city's wealth of attractions with one overriding question: What are the "Musts"?

To minimize the risk of selection, we provide a "condensed Paris" covering the various fields of interest. The sites listed below are those without which Paris has simply not been visited. Beside each suggested site is the tour route in this book where full details appear.

Museums

The Louvre: The largest art museum, with its glass pyramids. Le Premier *qurtier*. Palais du Louvre, Place du Carrousel and Louvre metro stations. Open daily 9:15am-5:15pm, closed Tues., tel. 42.60.39.26. (See "The Royal Heart of Paris").

Musée d'Orsay: Museum of Impressionism. 1 Place Henri de Montherlant. Solférino metro station. Open daily 10am-6pm, Thurs. until 9:45pm; closed Mon. (See "St.-Germain — Intellectuals and Aristocracy").

Centre Pompidou: Modern art center. 120 rue Saint-Martin. Hôtel de Ville and Rembuteau metro stations. Open Mon.-Fri. noon-10pm. Sat.-Sun. 10am-10pm; closed Tues. tel. 42.77.11.12. Admission: 20f, temporary exhibitions 16f; Sun. free. (See "Les Halles — Tomorrow's Paris").

Rodin: The best in sculpture. 77 rue de Varenne. Varenne metro station. Open daily 10am-5:15pm, closed Tues. tel. 47.05.01.34. Admission: 15f, Sun. free. (See "Les Invalides — an Empire Remembered").

De Cluny: Medieval exhibits. 6 Place Painlevé, 5e. Odéon or St-Michel metro station. Open daily 9:45am-12:30pm, 2-5pm, closed Tues. Admission: 9f, Sun. 4.50f. tel. 43.25.62.00. (See "The Latin Quarter with Latin Charm").

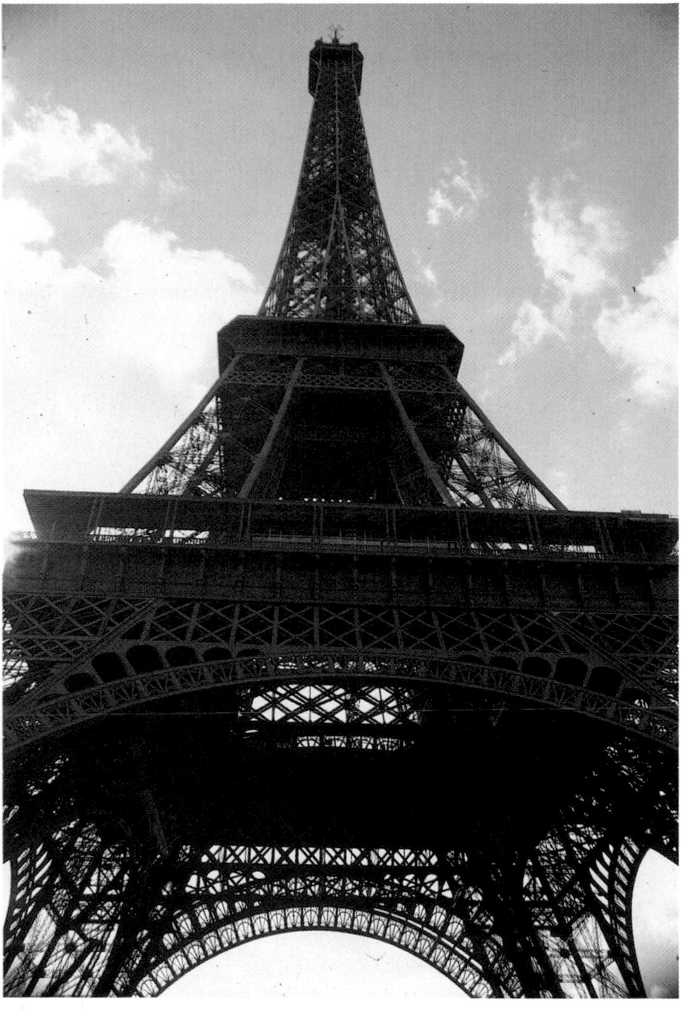

The Eiffel Tower — ten thousand tons of iron

Churches

Notre-Dame-de-Paris: The great cathedral. Place du Parvis-de-Notre-Dame. Ile de la Cité. Cité metro station. Open daily 10am-4:30pm. (See "The Islands — floating on the Seine").

St.-Chapelle: The most beautiful church. 4, bd. du Palais. Ile de la Cité. Cité metro station. Open daily 10am-5pm, tel. 43.54.30.09. (See "The Islands — floating on the Seine").

La Madeleine: A neo-classical church. Place de la Madeleine. La Madeleine metro station. Open daily 7:30am-7pm, tel 42.65.25.17. (See "L'Opéra and Cash Registers").

St.-Germain-des-Prés: A Gothic church. bd. St.-Germain corner. rue Bonaparte. St.-Germain-des-Prés metro station. Open 7:30am-7:45pm, Mon. open from 12:30pm (See "St.-Germain — Intellectuals and Aristocracy").

Monuments

La Tour Eiffel: Towering over Paris. Champ de Mars. Bior-Hakeim or RER C metro station. Open 10:30am-11pm, from 9:30am in summer. Admission: to first floor — 7f by stairs, 10f by elevator; to second floor — 22f by elevator; to third floor — 37f. (See "La Tour Eiffel").

Arc de Triomphe de l'Etoile: The grand arch. Place Charles de Gaulle (Place de l'Etoile). Ch. de Gaulle metro station. (See "Champs Elysées — Opulence and More Opulence").

Le Panthéon: A symbol to the French nation. Place du Panthéon, eastern exit of Jardins du Luxembourg. Luxembourg metro station. Open daily 10am-5pm, tel. 32.54.34.51. (See "The Latin Quarter with Latin Charm").

Les Invalides: A remnant of the Napoleonic Era. 2, Avenue de Tourville. La Tour Maubourg, metro station. Houses four museums. (See "Les Invalides — an Empire Remembered").

L'Opéra: A revival of the Second Empire. Place de l'Opéra. L'Opéra metro station. Open Mon.-Fri. 11am-4:30pm, tel. 42.66.50.22. (See "Opéra and Cash Registers")

City Sight

Champs Elysées: "The" Avenue. (See Champs Elysées — Opulence and More Opulence").

Place de la Concorde: An impressive plaza. (See "The Royal Heart of Paris").

The Latin Quarter: The "left bank". (See "The Latin Quarter with Latin Charm").

Place des Vosges: Festivities and outings. (See "Le Marais — Yesterday's Nobility").

Montmartre: The Paris of Toulouse-Lautrec. (See "Montmartre — the Rise and Fall of a Hill").

Shopping

Les Galeries Lafayette: 40, bd. Haussmann. Chaussée d'Antin metro station. Open Mon.-Sat. 9:30am-6:30pm, tel. 42.82.34.56. (See "L'Opéra and Cash Registers").

Le Printemps: 64, bd. Haussmann. Havre-Caumartin metro station. Open Mon.-Sat. 9:30-6:30, tel. 42.82.57.87. (See "Opéra and Cash Registers").

Montreuil: The flea market. Porte de Montreuil metro station. Open Sat.-Mon. morning to sunset. (See "Flea Markets — Bargain Hunting, Anyone?").

Making the Most of your Stay

Winning and Dining

Paris is a genuine paradise for food lovers who may choose from some 5,000 restaurants. The list of culinary styles is endless: traditional and modern French, Chinese, Japanese, Korean, Oriental, Italian, Portuguese, Russian, Polish, Jewish, Brazilian, African.

This Guide classifies them into three groups according to price. Quality and type are specified within each classification. Very expensive — an average of more than 300f per person; Expensive/Moderate — 150-300f; and Inexpensive — 50-150f. After listing the different French restaurants, there is a representative selection of restaurants offering cuisine from other countries.

Most restaurants open around noon and some stay open until 11pm or midnight. A few stay open later and others for 24-hours. For more popular restaurants, it is a good idea to reserve a table in advance. Otherwise, you may have to wait at the bar, sometimes for up to an hour, until a table becomes available.

Most restaurants offer a fixed-price menu along with a well-appointed à la carte menu, from which one chooses between two or three possibilities for each course. The fixed-price menu is the best way to keep costs down: the bill is known in advance, without surprises. In a deluxe restaurant where the average bill per meal comes to over 300f, for example, a fixed-price menu may be available for only 180f. The situation varies from one restaurant to another. Remember that the fixed-price menu may not include a dessert or drinks, which might explain why your bill suddenly seems a bit high.

For people who wish to enrich their culinary experience with extraordinary gastronomical moments, Paris is definitely the right place. Experts tend to regard French cuisine as the most interesting and superb. Paris offers a wonderful collection of restaurants with its many varieties and regional

Café Costes — very "in"

flavors (Normandy, Brittany, Alsace, etc.). This is the city for a wonderful excursion through the varieties and flavors of French cuisine. It need not cost too much either: many modest restaurants provide superb examples of the tradition, ability and professional aptitude of French chefs. The French regard "chefhood" as a tremendously respected profession. The chef is an artist, and his creations are works of art. The great chefs of the past century, Carême and Esoffier, are as universally familiar as those of our time, Paul Bocuse and Roger Verge.

These and others have successfully synthesized traditional cuisine with a modern approach to cooking which softens the rigid rules of the classic mode. This approach, called *nouvelle cuisine*, stresses the quality, freshness and variety of ingredients as the keys to rich flavor, precision of taste and the elegance and originality of the courses served. This is definitely not a "kitchen rebellion" but an adaptation of classical elements to modern demands. The great success of *nouvelle cuisine* has not come at the expense of classical Burgundy or cuisine regionale; these continue to flourish.

In recent years there has also been a proliferation of fast food restaurants in Paris. Their styles vary — hamburgers, french fries, hot dogs, pizza, etc. Kiosks serving sandwiches, omelets, pastry, etc., are also common.

"Institutes of Gastronomy" (over 300f per person)
Maxim's: 3, rue Royale, 8e, tel. 42.65.27.94. Concorde metro station. A few years ago, fashion designer Pierre Cardin bought the most famous restaurant in the western world and rescued it from a gradual decline into extinction. Today one can again ogle the international nobility of wealth while sitting back in red velvet seats, nibbling *nouvelle cuisine* delicacies and sipping top quality wines. Open till 1am; closed Sun.

La Tour d'Argent: 15, Quai de la Tournelle, 5e, tel. 43.54.23.31. Maubert-Mutualité metro station. Paris' oldest "gastronomical institute" has the most distinguished reputation in recent times. Its specialties include various delicacies of duck. Supreme among these is the world-famous *Duck in Orange*. Orders taken till 10pm; closed Mon. In 1988 another restaurant of the same name opened on Place de la Bastille, but the original resturant took them to court, and they had to change their name and pay a fine of 500,000f.

Lucas-Carton: 9, Place de la Madeleine, 8e, tel. 42.65.22.90. Madeleine metro station. Experts rate it today as one of the two or three best in Paris. The kitchen is orchestrated by one of the greatest chefs ever to hit France: Alain Sendersens, a true luminary of *nouvelle cuisine*. Such quality obviously translates into francs. A well-known Paris tale has it that a group of wealthy Americans dropped 55,000f in one evening. A modest eater can get out the door with an average of 900f, and a fixed-price menu at 600f is available as well. Orders taken until 10:30pm. Closed Sat. and Sun. Incidentally, in February 1989, Parisians got a shock to read that the restaurant had been sold by Alain Sendersens to Japanese business men from the *Sumitomo* group, for the amount of 40 million franc. They calmed down, however, when it was announced that Sendersens would continue to manage the restaurant.

La Coupole: 102, bd. Montparnasse, 14e, tel. 43.20.14.20. Vavin metro station. (See "Montparnasse — from Apollo to Hemingway".)

Robuchon: 32, rue de Longchamp, 16e, tel. 47.27.12.27. léna metro station. If a given restaurant is cited as "only" one of the two or three best in Paris, part of the reason is Robuchon. Many compliments are given for the unbelievably superb cuisine, the lovely old European decor and the imagination of this restaurant. Start with *crème de cauliflower* and continue with jellied caviar, peppered crab, cracked artichoke... Table service till 10:15pm. Closed Sat. and Sun.

Le Pré Catelan: rue de Suresnes, Bois de Boulogne, 16e, tel. 45.24.55.58. Within magnificent decor in the style of Louis XVI, alongside the beautiful greenery of Bois de Boulogne, you can enjoy superb cuisine which excels in exceptional and colorful dishes. Fish meals and meat delicacies with lots of imagination. The best of *nouvelle cuisine*. Closed Monday and Sunday afternoon. Service until 10pm.

Faugeron: 52, rue de Longchamps, 16e, tel. 47.04.24.53. léna metro station. The chef, Michel Faugeron, has earned many admirers through the marvelous delights which come out of his kitchen. Little new items appear on the menu, some of them even topical (ice cream shaped like the Louvre pyramids). Outstanding *nouvelle cuisine*, in slightly surrealistic blue decor. Excellent service. Closed Sat. and Sun. Service until 10pm.

Lasserre: 17, av. Franklin Roosevelt, 8e, tel. 43.59.53.43. One of the more classic resturants for traditional French cooking, for people with real class. For those who have never tasted lamb on a bed of endives or crab tails in sauce, and who have a special occasion to celebrate, this is the place to do so. Some claim that the prices are quite high in relation to the quality. Closed Monday afternoon and Sunday. Service until 10:30pm.

Ledoyen: 1, av. Dutuit, Carré des Champs-Elysées, 8e, tel. 47.42.57.84. Champs-Elysées metro station. One of the restaurants belonging to the famous Regine, queen of Paris night-life. Recently renovated and redesigned, it offers a varied classic bourgeois menu, with an emphasis on Mediterranean dishes with lots of cooked vegetables. Closed

Galeries Lafayette — sheer abundance

Sunday. Service until 10:30pm.

Olympe: 8, rue Nicolas Charlet, 15e, tel. 47.34.86.08. Pasteur metro station. A restaurant with real Parisian chic, haunt of the big names in the entertainment business. An excellent menu with less sophisticated but more generous French cuisine. A personal recommendation: minced brain in a spicy pastry. Closed Sat. and Sun. Service until midnight.

Lipp: 151, bd. Saint-Germain, 6e, tel. 45.48.53.91. St.-Germain-des-Prés metro station. One of the more distinguished names among the city's restaurants. A traditional favorite among politicians. For those who want to try excellent traditional, classic French cuisine. Open daily until 1am.

La Closerie Des Lilas: 171, bd. du Montparnasse, 6e, tel. 43.26.70.50. Vavin metro station. (See "Montparnasse — From Apollo to Hemingway".)

Gérard Besson: rue Coq-Héron, 1er, tel. 42.33.14.74. Les Halles metro station. Beneath beautiful chandeliers reflected in mirrors, chef Gérard Besson serves his delicious dishes in his personally created sauces, which are amazingly light. This is one of the up-and-coming restaurants in Paris, and its future seems very promising indeed. Closed Sunday. Service until 10pm.

Carré des Feuillants: 14, rue de Castaglione, 1er, tel. 42.86.82.82. Tuileries metro station. Truly excellent cuisine with a tendency towards south-west France, Gascon area. Wonderful escargot, asparagus with smoked ham. Lovers of Realist art can enjoy the posters of fruit and vegetable which adorn the walls. Closed Sat. afternoon and Sunday. Service until 10:30pm.

L'Ami Louis: 32, rue du Vertbois, 2e, tel. 48.87.77.48. Arts et Métiers metro station. A bistro with an established reputation and a charm of bygone days. A real experience to enjoy delicious food. Traditional bistro menu: beef ribs, roast chicken, fried mutton and lots of french fries. An absolute must for anyone who wants to specialize in the subject. Quite pricy. Closed Monday and Tuesday. Service until 10:30pm.

Lapérouse: 51, Quai des Grands Augustins, 6e, tel. 43.26.68.04. Saint Michel metro station. One of those places which time has not touched, bearing greeting from the end of the 19th century. This in itself justifies a visit, and that is even before tasting the classic cuisine with abundant sauces, amid a lively atmosphere. Closed Monday and Sunday afternoon. Service until 11:30pm.

Le Dôme: 108, bd. du Montparnasse, 14e, tel. 43.35.34.82. Vavin metro station. An establishment which does not need to rely on its respectable past and the famous names who dined there. (See "Montparnasse — From Apollo to Hemingway"). Offers wonderful *nouvelle cuisine* and some delicious surprises for lovers of seafood. The fish soup is recommended, as are most dishes here. Closed Monday. Service until 1pm.

Au Pressois: 257, av. Daumesnil, 12e, tel. 43.44.38.21. Porte Dorée metro station. The throngs who pass this restaurant on their way to the zoo, are doing themselves a real disservice by not stopping for a meal. Excellent *nouvelle cuisine*, with true inspiration from chef Henri Segvin. For lovers of *pâté de foie gras*, this is the place to experience the true wonders of this delicacy. Closed Sat. and Sun. Service until 10pm.

Le Toit de Passy: 94, av. Paul Doumer, 16e, tel. 45.24.55.37. Muette metro station. Located on the roof, this restaurant affords wonderful views of the surroundings. A favorite with real food lovers and gourmets, who come here for the *nouvelle cuisine* and remarkable wine cellar, with a selection to satisfy even the most descerning wine-lover. Closed Sat. afternoon and Sun. Service until 10:30pm.

Apicius: 43, av. des Ternes, 17e, tel. 43.80.19.66. Ternes metro station. Modern decor and wonderful cooking. The local chef, Jean-Pierre Vigato, is thought to be the rising star in the Parisian gastomonical sphere. For those who require proof, try the "lambs head" prepared with lemon, and for dessert the heavenly homemade ice-creams. Closed Sat. and Sun. Service until 10pm.

Jacques Cagna: 14, rue des Grands Augustins, 6e, tel. 43.26.49.39. Saint Michel metro station. If you want a taste of true aristocracy, something in the spirit of the pre-revolutionary nobilty, you can fulfil your wish at this renowned and established Paris institution. Superb *nouvelle cuisine*, in a classic atmosphere. Closed Sat. and Sun. Service until 10:30pm.

Good and interesting (150-300f per person)
Le Pressbourg: 3, av. de la Grande-Armée, 16e, tel. 45.00.24.77. Ch. de Gaulle-Etoile metro station. A modern restaurant with pleasant decor and a glass terrace opening onto the Arc de Triomphe. A varied menu of excellent seafood. Open daily and service until 1am.

Julien: 16, rue du Fg. St. Denis, 10e, tel. 47.70.12.06. Strasbourg St.-Denis metro station. This turn-of-the-century original decor can almost drive a person literally crazy. One does not know where to look — at the beautiful surroundings, the plate with its superb meat dishes, or the highly recommended, *cassoulet* (a French meat-and-bean casserole). Hopefully, you won't come on an evening with lots of noisy tourists. Open daily, service until 1:30am.

Chez Tante Madée: 11, rue Dupin, 6e, tel. 42.22.64.56. Sèvres Babylone metro station. A charming restaurant in a typical country French style, with superb classical cuisine. Its country-style chicken, served in a "fast-food" style, is unsurpassed anywhere. Incidentally, they bake their own bread which you can also order to take with you. Service till 10:30pm. Closed Sat. afternoon and Sun.

Le Verdois: 19, av. de la Motte-Picquet, 7^e, tel. 45.55.40.38. Ecole-Militaire metro station. Located between Les Invalides and bd. Marais museums and the Eiffel Tower — a strategic choice for those who explore Paris on foot. The superb menu includes mushrooms with spicy herbs, stuffed rabbit, hot oysters and mushrooms and whole-wheat blintzes. Closed Sun. Service until 11pm.

A la Grille Saint-Honoré: 15, Place du Marché-St.-Honoré, 1er, tel. 42.61.00.93. Pyramides metro station. Bistro-style restaurant with early 20th century atmosphere, serving excellent *nouvelle cuisine*. The artichoke and crab salad is particularly delicious, as are the desserts. Service until 10:30pm, closed Sun.

Daniel Tubuf: 26, rue de Montmorency, 3e, tel. 42.72.31.04. Arts et Métiers metro station. Restaurant with cuisine from Normandy region, offering an interesting and tasty selection of delicacies, with excellent wines and cheeses (for dessert). Recommended: marinated salmon, which brings out the best of this superb fish. Service until 10pm, closed Sat. and Sun.

La Guirlande de Julie: 25, Place des Vosges, 3e, tel. 48.87.94.07. Chemin Vert metro station. (see "Le Marais — Yesterday's Nobility").

Coconnas: 2, bis Place des Vosges, 3e, tel. 42.78.58.16. Vert Chemin metro station. One of the most highly recommended restaurants in the Les Marais *quartier*. An imaginative and varied menu. The tongue with cream and celery is a true delicacy. Excellent wines. Do not leave without trying the *Chocolate Marquise* for dessert. Service until 10:15pm, closed Mon. and Tues.

Le Caveau du Palais: 19, Place Dauphine, 1er, tel. 43.26.04.28. Pont Neuf metro station. (see "The Islands — "Floating" on the Seine".)

La Fermette du Sud-Ouest: 31, rue Coquillière, 1er, tel. 42.36.73.55. Les Halles metro station. Here you can taste the cuisine of the Périgord region without having to go down to south-west France. The salamis and sausages are delicious. Also worth trying is the aromatic *cassoulet* or the various duck dishes. Open daily, service until 10pm.

Le Globe d'Or: 158, rue St.-Honoré, 1er, tel. 42.60.23.37. Palais Royal metro station. Classical southern French cuisine, heavy but wonderfully tasty. The traditional *cassoulet* is outstanding. Service until 10:30pm, closed Sat. and Sun.

Pharamond: 24, rue de la Grande Truanderie, 1er, tel. 42.33.06.72. Les Halles metro station. An established institution with turn-of-the-century decor with the famous Normandy cuisine. It gained its renown for the remarkable *andouillette* (stuffed intestine) served here. The roasted pig's trotters are recommended. Service until 10:45pm, closed Sun. and Mon.

Gallopin: 40, rue Notre Dame des Victoires, 2e, tel. 42.36.45.38. Bourse metro station. Classical cuisine, 19th century decor and a very elegant clientele. The sole in cream sauce is an especially delicious dish. The house beer is particularly good. Service until 11pm, closed Sat. and Sun.

Bofinger: 3-7, rue de la Bastille, tel. 42.72.87.82. Bastille metro station. This is where the "big" names in entertainment and finance come to see and be seen, amid gorgeous mid-19th century decor. The house specialities are sauerkraut and frothy beer. It is usually crowded — but it's worthwhile. Open daily, service until 1am. A good place for dinner after an evening at the new Bastille Opera House.

Le Monde des Chimères: 69, rue St.-Louis en l'Ile, 4e, tel. 43.54.45.27. Sully Morland metro station. Ile St. Louis is always a pleasant place to visit, but especially so when dining in this charming restaurant. The interior is reminiscent of a medieval castle, with classical cuisine completing the effect. Try the chicken in garlic. Service until 10:30pm, closed Sun. and Mon.

La Bucherie: 41 rue de la Bucherie, 5e, tel. 43.54.78.06. Maubert-Mutualité metro station. After a tiring visit to Notre Dame, this is the place to dine. The excellent bourgeois cuisine deserves attention. Try the incomparable salmon soufflé. Open daily, service until 12:30am.

Diapason: 30, rue des Bernardins, 5e, tel. 43.54.21.13. Maubert-Mutualité metro station. A very elegant restaurant with an extremely pleasant atmosphere. For those who want to enjoy the famous french delicacy of frog legs, this is a house speciality. Service until 10:30pm, closed Sun. and Sat. afternoon.

Au Pactole: 44, bd. St.-Germain, 5e, tel. 46.33.31.31. Maubert-Mutualité metro station. Traditional classic cuisine, pleasant ambience and elegant decor. Succulent roast meats with delicious sauces. The *moules* (black oyster) soup is a wonderful experience. Service until 11pm, closed Sun. and Sat. afternoon.

Apollinaire: 168, bd. St.-Germain, 16e, tel. 43.26.50.30. St.-Germain-des-Prés metro station. A brasserie in turn-of-the-century style with excellent traditional fare. Leave some room for the cheeses and delicious desserts. Open daily, service until 11pm.

Good, interesting and affordable (50-140f per person)

Chartier: 7, rue du Fg. Montmartre, 9e, tel. 47.70.86.29. Rue Montmartre metro station. This is the best possible proof that one can eat well in surroundings of beauty and character without painful outlay of money. The *fin de siècle* decor features cluster chandeliers and a glass ceiling. The cuisine is classical French, the price level stubbornly low. Should be considered a "must" on a visit to Paris. Open daily and service until 9:30pm.

Polidor: 41, rue Monsieur-le-Prince, 6e, tel. 43.26.95.34. Odéon metro station. Old furniture and linoleum from the pre-war era combine here with homey, bourgeois cuisine. *Polidor* has attracted a clientele of artists, poets and authors for several decades, including James Joyce who was a regular customer. There is a very special atmosphere and there is a determined effort to keep the prices down. The guinea fowl with cabbage is particularly delicious. Service till 1am, and on Sunday until 10pm.

La Casa Miguel: 48, rue St.-Georges, 9e, tel. 42.81.09.61. St.-Georges metro station. Truly out-of-this-world: the cheapest meal in town (possibly even the whole of Western Europe) for about 40 years. Starter, main course, dessert, wine and bread... for 5f. (that's no typo!). Open noon-1pm, 7-8pm, closed Sunday evenings. Definitely a piece of Paris folklore.

Le Gros Minet: 1, rue des Prouvaires, 1er, tel. 42.33.03.62. Les Halles metro station. A lively restaurant (much like the mood of the house accordianist), which serves generous and tasty servings of classical French cuisine, with a tendency towards simplicity. The lunch menu is interesting and inexpensive. Closed Mon., Sat. and Sun. for lunch. Service until 10pm.

L'Incroyable: 26, rue Richelieu, 1er, tel. 42.96.24.64. Palais Royal metro station. Next to the Louvre, this restaurant is ideal for a relaxing meal after a tiring day at the museum. It is a bistro serving classical popular and inexpensive fare. Closed Mon. and Sat. night and Sun.

Lescure: 7, rue de Mondovi, 1er, tel. 42.60.18.91. Concorde metro station. (see "The Royal Heart of Paris".)

Le Brissemoret: 5, rue Saint-Marc, 2e, tel. 42.36.91.72. Montmartre metro station. A small, pleasant bistro with a family atmosphere. Good classic French cuisine. A local combination is recommended: lamb chops with one of the excellent red wines on the menu. Service until 10:30pm. Closed Saturday and Sunday.

La Criée: 31, bd. Bonne Nouvelle, 2e, tel. 42.33.32.99. Bonne Nouvelle metro station. There are two other restaurants of this chain in Paris: 84 bd. du Montparnasse, 15e and 15, rue Lagrange, 5e. For lovers of sea food. The name of the game here is the quick service, reasonable prices and excellent selection of fish prepared in a variety of ways. Open daily, service until 1am.

Chez Jenny: 39, bd. du Temple, 3e, tel. 42.74.75.75. République metro station. A famous and successful Alsace restaurant (meaning that you must book a table or wait for one). Serves superb Alsace sauerkraut amid Alsacian decor. The mussels are extremely popular. Open daily, service until 1am.

Zéro de Conduite: 66, rue Monsieur le Prince, 6e, tel. 43.54.50.79. Odéon metro station. A charming restaurant for visitors and residents of the Latin Quarter, with a large selection of roast meats: pork, veal, chicken and more. The varied menu also has the North African specialty — *couscous*. Open daily.

La Fontaine de Mars: 129, rue Saint-Dominique, 7e, tel. 47.05.56.44. Ecole Militaire metro station. A real find for lovers of traditional French family-style cuisine. Simple and tasty fare. The atmosphere, decor and even the prices belong to the past. Try and save some room for the house pastries. Closed Saturdays and Sun. night. Service until 10pm.

La Petite Chaise: 36, rue de Grenelle, 7e, tel. 42.22.13.35. Sèvres Babylone metro station. A wonderful example of continuity: this restaurant opened in 1680! It is still charming, offering traditional cuisine in a special atmosphere. The trout is particularly recommended. Open daily, service until 11pm.

Taverne Kronenbourg: 24, bd. des Italiens, 9e, tel. 47.70.16.64. Opéra metro station. A typical bustling Alsace tavern, with a regular menu and band. Relatively inexpensive with good food. Sauerkraut of course, and excellent beer, sea food (the trout in white wine is excellent). Also serves meat grilled over a fire. Open daily, service until 2am.

Aux Artistes: 63, rue Falguière, 14e, tel. 43.22.05.39. Pasteur metro station. As its name indicates, this is a meeting place of artists (depending on the day), with a relatively inexpensive menu. Quality traditional cuisine, and an extensive selection of entrees and main dishes. The local *boeuf bourguignon* is particularly recommended. Service until 1am, closed Sunday.

Bistrot Champêtre: 107 rue Saint-Charles, 15e, tel. 45.77.85.06. Charles Michel metro station. A pleasant restaurant, combining old and new — traditional cuisine with a modern approach. An inexpensive fixed-menue for lunch, including delicacies such as smoked salmon. Delicious fish and excellent wines. Open daily, service until 11pm.

Le Connétable: 55, rue des Archives, 3e, tel. 42.77.41.40. Hôtel de Ville metro station. This restaurant serves as a good break while touring around the Les Marais quarter. Pleasant atmosphere, antique decor in the style of the area and fairly good traditional cuisine with an inexpensive fixed-menu. Roast lamb chops recommended. Service until midnight. Closed Sat. and Sun.

La Cantine: 245, bis, rue St. Jacques, 5e, tel. 43.26.97.92. Luxembourg metro station. The speciality of the house is fish, prepared in a number of outstanding dishes. There is more besides fish on the menu, though it is best to stick to the fish. The fixed-menu is reasonably priced. Service until 10pm, closed Sun. and Mon.

Perraudin: 157, rue St.-Jacques, 5e, tel. 46.33.15.75. Maubert-Mutualité metro station. Classical French cuisine, old-fashioned and generous style. A pleasant place popular with students, not only because of its proximity to the Sorbonne and its reasonable prices. Service until 10:15pm, closed Saturday.

L'Assiette au Bœuf: 22, rue Guillaume Appollinaire, 6e, tel. 42.60.88.44. St.-Germain-des-Prés metro station. For lovers of good but simple meat dishes. This is the place for an excellent piece of beef, served with french fries made just the way they should be. Efficient service and a continuous high standard. Open daily, service until 1am.

La Boutique aux Sandwichs: 12, rue du Colisée, 8e, tel. 43.59.56.69. St.-Philippe-du-Roulle metro station. (See "Champs-Elysées — Opulence and More Opulence".)

Hippopotamus: 6 av. Franklin Roosevelt, 8e, tel. 42.25.77.96. Franklin Roosevelt metro station. The first restaurant of a chain of which has sprung up all over the city over the past twenty years. The principle here is simple: roast meats, juicy steaks (standard varies), salads and dessert. The menu is relatively inexpensive and the service quick and efficient. Open daily, service until 1am.

Folk food — in a nutshell

This sub-chapter is devoted to foreign cuisine in Paris. There is nothing better than an exceptional folk restaurant:

Sweet World Cafe: 161, rue Montmartre, 2e, tel. 42.33.77.62. Rue Montmartre metro station. This huge place, until recently a complex of a number of movie theaters, has become a movieland restaurant — lively decor, modern and young in spirit, honey-colored lighting and beautiful waitresses. On each table are huge round menus, which actually comprise no less than seven different menus, with seven different types of national cuisine from around the world — French, American, Chinese, Haitian, Mexican, Swedish and Italian. Diners can create an international meal for themselves — a French entree, a Swedish main course, and a Chinese dessert. Everything is of a high standard and the prices are reasonable, between 150-200f per person. Can be less depending on what one orders. Open daily, service until 1am.

The restaurants which appear here according to nationality are also arranged into three categories, like their French counterparts: Expensive — above 300f per person; moderate — 150-300f per person and inexpensive — between 50-150f per person.

Chinese — Vietnamese
Bonsai: 23, av. Victoria, 1er, tel. 42.36.81.12. Châtelet metro station. Inexpensive. Open daily until 12:15am.
Tong-Yen: 1 bis, rue Jean Mermoz, 8e, tel. 42.25.04.23. Franklin Roosevelt metro station. Moderate. Closed Sat. afternoon and Sun. Service until midnight.
Descartes Mandarin: 31, rue Descartes, 5e, tel. 43.25.55.21. Monge metro station. Inexpensive. Closed Sat. afternoon and Sun. Service until 11pm.
Tan-Dinh: 60, rue de Verneuil, 7e, tel. 45.44.04.84. Solférino metro station. Moderate. Closed Sun. Service until 11pm.

Japanese
Edo: 42, rue Sainte-Anne, 2e, tel. 42.96.69.81. Quatre Septembre metro station. Expensive. Service until 10:30pm. Closed Tues.
Akasaka: 9, rue Nicolo, 16e, tel. 42.88.77.86. Passy metro station. Expensive. Service until 11pm. Closed Sun. evenings.
Matsuda: 13, rue de Helder, 9e, tel. 47.70.40.91. Chaussée d'Antin metro station. Moderate. Service until 10:30pm. Closed Sat. afternoon and Sun.
E.Bi.Su: 7, rue Royer-Collard, 5e, tel. 43.26.80.35. Inexpensive. Service until 11:30pm. Closed Sun. and Mon.

Spanish
Au Derric Catalan: 346, rue Lecourbe, 15e, tel. 45.58.48.75. Balard metro station. Moderate. Service until 10pm. Closed Mon.
La Paëlla: 50, rue des Vinaigriers, 10^{e}, tel. 42.08.28.89. Jacques-Bonsergent metro station. Moderate. Open daily, service until 1am.
Roberto: 8, rue des Tournelles, 4°, tel. 42.77.48.37. Bastille metro station. Inexpensive. Service until 11pm. Closed Sun.
Casa Pepe: 5, rue Mouffetard, 5^{e}, tel. 43.54.97.33. Monge metro station. Moderate. Open daily, service until 2:30am.

Italian
Il Teatro: 60, bd. du Montparnasse, 15^{e}, tel. 45.48.20.60. Montparnasse metro station. Inexpensive. Open daily, service until midnight.
Villa Medicis: 11, rue St.-Placide, 6e, tel. 42.22.51.96. St.-Placide metro station. Moderate. Service until 11pm. Closed Sun.
La Tavola: 10, rue de la Roquette, 11e, tel. 47.00.20.85. Bastille metro station. Inexpensive. Open daily, service until 1am.
La Main à la Pâte: 35, rue St.-Honoré, 1er, tel. 45.08.85.73. Les Halles metro station. Expensive. Service until 12:30am. Closed Sun.

Polish
Cracovia: 33, av. Philippe-Auguste, 11e, tel. 43.70.36.72. Nation metro station. Moderate. Closed Sun.
Wanouchka: 28, rue de la Vieuville, 18e, tel. 42.57.36.15. Abbesses metro station. Moderate. Only open in the evening, closed Wed. Service until 11pm.
Polonus: 130, rue Cardinet, 17e, tel. 40.54.01.28. Malesherbes metro station. Inexpensive. Open daily, service until 11pm.

Russian
Karlov: 197, rue de Grenelle, 7e, tel. 45.51.29.21. La Tour-Maubourg metro station. Moderate. Service until 11:30pm. Closed Sun.
Mignonnette du Caviar: 13, rue du Colisée, 8e, tel. 42.25.30.35. St.-Philippe du Roule metro station. Inexpensive. Service until 11pm. Closed Sun. and Sat. afternoon.
Anna Karenina: 176, rue St.-Martin, 3e, tel. 48.04.03.63. Rambuteau metro station. Moderate. Open every evening, service until 2am.
Dominique: 19, rue Bréa, 6e, tel. 43.27.08.80. Vavin metro

station. Moderate. Open daily, service until 10:15pm.

North African

Chez Léon: 11, bd. Beaumarchais, 4e, tel. 42.78.42.55. Bastille metro station. Inexpensive. Tunisian cuisine. Open daily, service until 11:30pm.

Marrakech: 12, rue d'Armaillé, 17e, tel. 43.80.26.65. Argentine metro station. Moderate. Moroccan cuisine. Only open in the evenings, closed Mon. Service until 11pm.

Le Mazafran: 7, rue Corneille, 6e, tel. 43.26.03.65. Luxembourg metro station. Inexpensive. Service until 10:30pm. Closed Sun.

Station Nord-Est: 15, rue du 8 Mai 1945, 10e, tel. 40.37.74.16. Gare de l'Est metro station. Inexpensive. Open daily, service until 5am!

South American

Azteca: 7, rue Sauval, 1er, tel. 42.36.11.16. Les Halles metro station. Inexpensive. Mexican cuisine. Service until midnight. Closed Sun.

Copacabana: 281, rue Lecourbe, 15e, tel. 45.54.60.98. Boucicaut metro station. Inexpensive. Brazilian cuisine. Service until 11:30pm. Closed Sun. and Mon.

Machu-Picchu: 9, rue Royer-Collard, 5e, tel. 43.26.13.13. Luxembourg metro station. Moderate. Peruvian cuisine. Open evenings only, closed Sun. Service until 11pm.

Guy: 6, rue Mabillon, 6e, tel. 43.54.87.61. Mabillon metro station. Moderate. Brazilian cuisine. Open evenings, closed Sun. Service until 1am.

Light Meals

Life outside the restaurant: Paris' cafes serve highly commendable light meals. They save the visitor time, money and sometimes a few calories, adding a special atmosphere of bustle — people coming, going, having fun living. And most importantly, cafes are found everywhere, on every corner of every street — wherever you turns

Try breakfast at one of these, instead of a hotel where one might share a dining room with the walls. Snap up a light lunch *en route* to a tour. Cap your day there, before or after a night's entertainment (most cafes stay awake from dawn to the wee hours). Sip some lemonade, beer or wine at the counter (less expensive) or at a table. Slip a coin into a juke box and add some musical accompaniment. This is a true Paris cafe — one of local society's important institutions.

Some of the major ingredients in the cafe menu should be mentioned:
croque-monsieur: grilled cheese with ham.
croque-madame: as above, crowned with a sunny-side-up egg.
hot dog: sausage in a bun, topped with yellow cheese.
gruyère beurre: yellow cheese in a buttered baguette (long French bread).
jambon beurre: ham in a buttered baguette.
rillettes: a delicious but quite greasy pork or goose "paté".
saucisson sec-à l'ail: plain or garlic-flavored sausage in a baguette.
camembert beurre: camembert cheese and butter in a baguette.
croissant: flaky crescent-shaped roll.
petit pain au chocolat: like a croissant, but with a vein of chocolate in the middle.

Tea Salons

An institution in themselves, tea salons, *salon de thé*, are where people come to enjoy hot chocolate, excellent coffee, tea and delicious cakes. Those who understand French can pick up interesting tidbits of news, as tea salons are a favorite Parisian meeting place to sit and gossip. The following lists includes some of the more prominent of these institutions. Most also serve light meals.

Angélina: 226, rue de Rivoli, 4e, tel. 42.60.82.00. Concorde metro station.
L'Arbre à Cannelle: 57, Passage des Panoramas, 1er, tel. 45.08.55.87. Bourse metro station.
Rose-Thé: 91, rue Saint Honoré, 1er, tel. 42.36.97.18. Louvre metro station.
Pandora: 24, passage Choiseul, 2e, tel. 47.42.07.19. Quatre-Septembre metro station.
Marais Plus: 20, rue des Francs Bourgeois, 3e, tel. 42.72.73.52. Saint-Paul metro station.
La Charlotte de l'Isle: rue Saint Louis en l'Ile, 4e, tel. 43.54.25.83. Pont Marie metro station.
Sweet et Faim: 1 rue de la Bûcherie, 5e, tel. 43.25.82.16. Maubert-Mutualité metro station.

Brunch

On Sundays many regular restaurants are closed, in addition to which, this is day of the week to sleep away the morning. Parisians and many tourists visiting the city have found a solution to this by eating brunch — a combined breakfast and lunch. The following is a list of establishments which serve a good brunch, for about 100f per person.

Smith and Son: 248, rue de Rivoli, 1er, tel. 42.60.37.97. Concorde metro station.
Olsson's: 62, rue Pierre-Charron, 8e, tel. 45.61.49.11. Franklin Roosevelt metro station.
Al Goldenberg: 60, av. de Wagram, 8e, tel. 42.27.34.79. Ternes metro station.
L'Aviatic: 23, rue Ste.-Groix-de-la Bretonnerie, 4e, tel. 42.78.26.20. Hôtel de Ville metro station.
Le Cactus Bleu: 8, rue de Lappe, 11e, tel. 43.28.30.20. Bastille metro station.
Eurydice: 10, Pl. des Vosges, 4e, tel. 42.77.77.99. Chemin Vert metro station.
King Opéra: 21, rue Daunou, 2e, tel. 42.60.99.89. Opéra metro station.

Filling the Basket: Where to Shop for What

Paris can satisfy anyone on a shopping spree. Department stores, shopping centers and a myriad of shops of all types and sizes tempt locals and visitors alike.

The best and most successful shopping, at the most interesting prices, is usually the result of lots of legwork and a bit of luck. An important rule, of course, is the motto of every consumer protection society: shop around.

Department stores and shopping centers cut many kilometers of walking off shopping expeditions. Be aware, however, that the prices in such establishments are high, though not exorbitant. There's no room here for bargain hunting or, of course, bargaining. The exception to this is the *soldes*, which are clearance sales, when prices are significantly lower. These take place in January after the holidays and the summer sales are in July. During the course of the year, there are irregular discounts on certain items.

Detaxe — Duty Free Shops

All tourists over the age of 15, who stay in France for less than six months, are permitted to make duty free purchases. The customs exemption does apply to most items, but there are some exceptions: foodstuffs, tobacco, medicines, weapons, gold, unset precious stones, antiques and works of art (unless with special permission) and motor vehicles. The other proviso is that purchases are not in commercial quantities, and that the tourist is able to carry the articles within his personal baggage upon leaving the country.

In the department stores or shops that deal with *detaxe*, the salesman fills out a special form in triplicate, two pink and one green at the time of purchase. You need to present your passport at the store. Upon leaving the country, present the goods purchased to the customs clerk (at the special counter before passing through the border police), along with the forms and stamped envelope which you received in the store.

The clerk takes the pink copies, leaving you with the green form. There are several ways the money can be returned to you: you can get it in cash from one of the airport banks, or it can be deposited directly into your account through your credit card, or sent to your home address. The choice is yours. The minimum amount on purchases in order to get a *detaxe* refund is 1200f (irrespective of the number of purchases), and the refund varies from item to item.

In addition to the department stores which have special counters which deal with *detaxe*, certain stores also specialize in duty free sales to tourists. They also offer special reductions at the time of purchase — and it is usually worthwhile doing your shopping there. They stock mainly perfumes, cosmetics, leather goods, exclusive clothing, gifts, etc. The most popular are:

Raoul et Curly: 47, av. de l'Opéra, 2ᵉ. Opéra metro station.
Michel Swiss: 16, rue de la Paix, 2ᵉ. Opera metro station.
Paris Opéra: 16, av. de l'Opéra, 1ᵉʳ. Palais-Royal metro station.
Liza: 42, av. Kléber, 16ᵉ, Kléber metro station.
Eiffel Shopping: 9, av. de Suffren, 7ᵉ. Bir-Hakeim metro station.
For You: 380, rue Saint-Honoré, 1ᵉʳ. Concorde metro station.

Department Stores

They have almost everything imaginable, including bars, restaurants, and services ranging from shoe repair to travel agencies. Though large department stores have smaller branches elsewhere in Paris, the main outlets are the major attractions. Below is a list of major department stores. Details for the larger stores appear in the tour routes.

Galeries Lafayette: 40, bd. Haussmann, 9ᵉ. Chaussée d'Antin metro station.
BHV: 52, rue de Rivoli, 4ᵉ. Hôtel de Ville metro station.
Au Bon Marché: 2, rue de Sèvres, 7ᵉ. Sèvres Babylone metro station.
Le Printemps: 64, bd. Haussmann, 9ᵉ. Havre-Caumartin metro station.
La Samaritaine: 91, rue de la Monnaie, 1ᵉʳ. Pont Neuf metro station.
FNAC: 136, rue de Rennes, 6ᵉ. Montparnasse metro station. (books, records, cameras, electronics).
Marks and Spencer: 35, bd. Haussmann, 9ᵉ. Havre-Caumartin metro station.

Aux Trois Quartiers: 17, bd. de la Madeleine, 1er. Madeleine metro station.

Shopping Centers

These are literally miniature cities of commerce — sheltered, air conditioned and wallet-tempting. They include shops of every type and hue, and a variety of leisure possibilities.

Centre Commercial Beaugrenelle: Place Fernand-Forest, 15^{e}. Charles-Michel metro station.
Centre Galaxie: 30, av. d'Italie, 13^{e}. Place d'Italie metro station.
Centre Maine-Montparnasse: Tour Montparnasse, 14^{e}. Montparnasse metro station.
Arcades de Montmartre: Place Clichy, 18^{e}. Place Clichy metro station.
Forum des Halles: rue Berger, 1er. Les Halles metro station.

Shops

Good shopping is a matter of skill. But here, too, a little help does not hurt. The lists below answer various tastes — luxury, bargain and the range in between. The selection reflects Parisian standards; goods advertised as "bargains" in Paris may show up at home as luxury items. The lists are categorized by type of shop and price level.

Women's fashions

Expensive — luxury shops

The place to go: **Faubourg Saint-Honoré**. This is where princesses, or at least millionaires, top up their wardrobes. Even low-budget visitors, however, have the right to satiate their curiosity.

Christian Dior: 30, av. Montaigne, 8e, tel. 47.23.54.44. Franklin D. Roosevelt metro station.
Lanvin: 22, Fg.-St.-Honoré, 8e, tel. 42.65.14.40. Madeleine metro station.
Nina Ricci: 39, av. Montaigne, 8e, tel. 47.23.78.88. Franklin D. Roosevelt metro station.
Yves Saint-Laurent: 5, av. Marceau, 16e, tel. 47.23.72.71. Alma Marceau metro station.
Chanel: 31, rue Cambon, 1er, tel. 42.61.54.55. Madeleine metro station.
Christian Lacroix: 73, rue du Fg.-St.-Honoré, 8e, tel. 42.65.79.08. Madeleine metro station.

Jean-Paul Gaultier: 6, rue Vivienne, 2e, tel. 42.86.05.05. Richelieu-Drouot metro station.
Montana: 3, rue des Petits-Champs, 1er, tel. 40.20.02.14. Bourse metro station.
Thierry Mugler: 49, av. Montaigne, 8e, tel. 47.23.37.62. Franklin D. Roosevelt metro station.

Good shops at reasonable prices
The places to go: **Les Halles**, **St.-Germain**.
Anastasia: 18, rue de l'Ancienne Comédie, 6e, tel. 43.25.33.65. Odéon metro station.
Cacharel: 34, rue Tronchet, 9e, tel. 47.42.11.46. Madeleine metro station.
Benetton: 63, rue de Rennes, 6e, tel. 45.48.80.92. St.-Sulpice metro station.
La Nacelle: 8, Places des Victoires, 1er, tel. 42.96.03.27. 4-Septembre metro station.
Ulpa: 17, rue des Halles, 1er, tel. 42.61.49.96. Les Halles metro station.

Inexpensive
Bargains are usually low-price, high-quality merchandise with the manufacturers' labels removed. Sometimes, though, goods with minor defects do show up. *Caveat emptor*. The best areas to wander around for bargains are **rue d'Alésia** and **rue St-Placide**. For "junky" clothes at bargain prices try the area around the **Barbès-Rochechouart** metro station.

Le Mouton à Cinq Pattes: 8, 10, 48, rue St.-Placide, 6e, tel. 45.48.86.26. St.-Placide metro station.
Turbigo 11: 11, rue de Turbigo, 1er, tel. 45.08.92.30. Etienne Marcel metro station.
Revoir: 31, rue de la Ferronnerie, 1er, tel. 45.08.80.07. Châtelet metro station.
La Redoute: Forum des Halles, 3, Place Carrée. Les Halles metro station.

Men's Fashions

Altona: 6, rue de l'Odéon, 6e, tel. 43.26.31.61. Odéon metro station.
Arnys: 14, rue de Sèvres, 7e, tel. 45.48.76.99. Sèvres Babylone metro station.
Charvet: 28, Place Vendôme, 1er, tel. 42.60.30.70. Opéra metro station.

Ivy Oxford: 6, rue Brantome, 3e, tel. 42.71.09.77. Rambuteau metro station.
Jarvys: 48-50 Galerie Vivienne, 2e, tel. 42.97.49.03. Bourse metro station.

Footwear

Expensive — luxury shops
Céline: 3, av. Victor Hugo, 16e, tel. 45.01.79.41. Etoile metro station.
Clarence: 104, av. des Champs-Elysées, 8e, tel. 45.62.75.19. Georges V metro station.
Maud Frizon: 83, rue des St.-Pères, 6e, tel. 42.22.06.93. St.-Sulpice metro station.
Sacha: 24, rue de Buci, 6e, tel. 43.54.43.50. St.-Germain-des-Prés metro station.
Weston: 114, av. des Champs-Elysées, 8e, tel. 45.62.26.47. Georges V metro station.

Moderate
Bally: 156, rue de Rivoli, 1er, tel. 42.60.22.46. Louvre metro station, (belongs to a chain).
Xavier Danaud: 78, rue des Sts.-Pères, 7e, tel. 45.48.55.71. Sèvres Babylone metro station.
Charles Jourdan: 7, rue Pierre Lescot, 1er, tel. 42.97.50.70. Châtelet metro station.
Manfield: 146, rue de Rennes, 6e, tel. 45.48.83.21. St.-Placide metro station, (belongs to a chain).
Salamander: 53, bd. St.-Michel, 5e, tel. 43.54.10.20. Luxembourg metro station.

Inexpensive
André: 102, av. des Champs-Elysées, 8e, (belongs to a chain).
Bata: 68, rue de Rivoli, 4e (belongs to a chain).
Eram: 144, rue de Rivoli, 1er, (belongs to a chain).
Myrys: 91, rue de Rivoli, 1er, (belongs to a chain).
Freeshoes: 78, rue De Rivoli, 1er, tel. 48.87.63.26. Châtelet metro station.
L'Année Dernière: 26, rue de la Grande Truanderie, 1er, tel. 42.36.35.06. Les Halles metro station.

Bargains
Berny's: 9, rue Vavin, 6e, tel. 43.26.63.84. Vavin metro station.
Chiche: 38, rue de Berri, 8e, tel. 45.63.49.50. Georges V metro station.

Gianni: 28, rue des Mathurins, 9e, tel. 42.68.13.92. Havre Caumartin metro station.

Jewelry

Expensive — luxury shops
The place to go: **Place Vendôme**.

Boucheron: 26, Place Vendôme, 1er, tel. 42.61.58.16. Opéra metro station.
Cartier: 13, rue de la Paix, 1er, tel. 42.61.58.36. Opéra metro station.
Maubussin: 20, Place Vendôme, 1er, tel. 42.60.44.93. Opéra metro station.
Van Cleef & Arpels: 22, Place Vendôme, 1er, tel. 42.61.58.58. Opéra metro station.

Moderate
Jean Vêndome: 352, rue St.-Honoré, 1er, tel. 42.60.88.34.
Fred: 6, rue Royale, 8e, tel. 42.60.30.65.
Técla: 2, rue de la Paix, 2e.

Inexpensive
Agatha: Forum des Halles, Niveau 2, 1er, tel. 42.97.42.88, (belongs to a chain).

Corium: 46, rue Croix des Petits Champs, 1er, tel. 42.61.29.24.
Fabrice: 33, rue Bonaparte, 6e, tel. 43.26.57.95.
Utility-Bibi: 27, rue Dufour, 6e, tel. 43.25.53.77.
Burma: 15, bd. de la Madeleine, 1er, tel. 42.61.11.63. Specializes in cheap imitations of expensive jewelry.

Handbags, Belts and Leather Goods

Expensive — luxury shops
Gucci: 2 & 27, rue du Fg. St.-Honoré, 1er, tel. 42.96.83.27. Madeleine metro station.
Hermès: 24 rue, du Fg. St.-Honoré, 1er, tel. 42.65.21.60. Madeleine metro station.
Lancel: 43, rue de Rennes, 6e, tel. 42.22.94.73. St.-Germain-des-Prés metro station.
Louis Vuitton: 78 Bis, av. Marceau, 8e, tel. 47.20.47.00. Ch. de Gaulle-Etoile metro station.

Moderate
La Bagagerie: 41, rue du Four, 6e, tel. 45.48.85.88. Mabillon metro station.

Question de Peaux: 6, rue de Monfaucon, 6e, tel. 43.54.09.93.
Upla: 17, rue des Halles, 1er, tel. 42.61.49.96.

Beauty

(beauty salons which also sell cosmetic products)

Carita: 11, rue du Fg. St.-Honoré, 8e, tel. 42.65.79.00.
Clarins: 35, rue Tronchet, 8e, tel. 42.65.30.70.
Guerlain: 68, av. des Champs-Elysées, 8e, tel. 43.59.31.10.
Revlon: 95, av. des Champs-Elysées, 8e, tel. 47.23.71.44.

Hair Salons

Most Paris barbershops appear to be reliable, clean and trouble-free. The following are "big names" with down-to-earth prices:

Alexandre: 3, av. Matignon, 8e, tel. 42.25.57.90.
Jean Louis David: 47, rue Pierre Charron, 8e, tel. 43.59.75.16.
Harlow: 24, rue St. Denis, 1er, tel. 42.33.61.36.
Jacques Dessange: 37, av. Franklin-Roosevelt, 8e, tel. 43.59.31.31.
Maniatis: 18, rue Marbeuf, 8e, tel. 47.23.30.14.
Mod's Hair: 7, rue de Ponthieu, 8e, tel. 43.59.06.50.

Gifts

Dyptique: 34, bd. St.-Germain, 5e, tel. 43.26.45.27. Maubert-Mutualité metro station.
La Palme: 136, rue St.-Honoré, 8e, tel. 43.59.03.82. St.-Philippe du Roule metro station.
L'Entrepot: 50, rue de Passy, 16e, tel. 45.25.64.17. Muette metro station.
Catherine-Prou: 18, rue Mesnil, 16e, tel. 47.27.77.87. Victor Hugo metro station.
Aux Etats Unis: 229, rue St.-Honoré, 1er, tel. 42.66.73.95. Tuileries metro station, (walking sticks).

Posters, Postcards and Photos

Le Chapitre: 23, rue Guénégaud, 6e, tel. 43.54.27.70. Odéon metro station.
Images d'Epinal: 14, rue des Jardins St.-Paul, 4e, tel. 42.71.55.10. Pont Marie metro station.
Le Zinzin d'Hollywood: 5, rue de Condé, 5e, tel. 43.54.66.80. Odéon metro station.

Tobacconists

A La Civette: 157, rue St.-Honoré, 1er, tel. 42.96.04.99. Palais Royal metro station.
Au Caïd: 24, bd. St.-Michel, 6e, tel. 43.26.04.01. St.-Michel metro station.

Entertainment

How does one spend an evening in Paris? Answering this is like having a botanist explain what grows in the equatorial jungles. Paris tries to live up to one of its more obligatory nicknames, the City of Lights, and to maintain a very high level of activity during prime-time entertainment hours.

To keep abreast of everything, consult the three high-circulation weekly publications which appear at any Paris newsstand every Wednesday — *Pariscope* (3f), *L'Officiel* (2f) and *7 à Paris* (6f). Rudimentary French is sufficient.

A relatively new concept in Paris is the *Kiosque Théâtre* (Theatre Kiosks). There are two such kiosks operating in the city today, at Place de la Madeleine and in the R.E.R. station at Châtelet-Les-Halles. These operate on the same principle of those in New York and London, where you can get tickets for shows at half-price on the day of the show. The service includes theater, opera, ballet, concerts, clubs, etc. The two kiosks are open daily from 12:45-7pm, and usually have tickets to over 120 different shows around the city.

The survey below lists the entertainment options by type, mentioning some of the most important and conspicuous establishments. For specific programs on particular dates, consult local publications or the Bureau du Tourisme.

Cinema

Almost all Paris' cinemas screen several movies at once in individual halls. Recently, there has been a tendency to return to large movie theaters, with huge screens and sophisticated sound systems. It is really worth trying to catch a movie at one of new cinemas. Particularly recommended is *Max Linder*: 24, bd. Poissonnière. Films are usually shown here in their original language. Movie titles are displayed at the cashier, together with the times when tickets go on sale for each film (tickets cannot be bought in advance and each screening is booked separately). These are called *séances*. The film begins after 15-25 minutes of commercials, short films, or coming attractions. After buying a ticket one is seated by an usher wherever *she* pleases. One can insist on another seat. The usher is given a tip of 2-3f, or so, in any event. Non-tippers get a dirty look, for good reason, under local norms.

Ticket prices hover around 35f, depending on location. Cinemas around Champs-Elysées are the most expensive and those in the outer *quartiers* are the least so. Student cards produce discounts up to 30% in some Paris cinemas. On Monday nights, there is a general reduction of about 10f (at least) on all tickets.

Note: The letters *V.O.* beside the name of a film indicate that the film is being shown in its original language with French translation. *V.F.* indicates that the film has been dubbed into French. Most films appear simultaneously at several cinemas, enabling one to choose *V.F.* or *V.O.*, as desired.

The Paris Cinémathèque has two theaters in different parts of town — one in the cinema museum at Palais de Chaillot, the other in the Pompidou Center (see tour routes for details). They show four different films each day. Ticket: 16f.

Nightclubs

The great nightclubs of Paris, those which put on large-scale showcase performances, full of shapely dancers and ostrich feathers, are renowned worldwide. They've maintained their spectacular effects... and prices. Though the programs change every few years, the principle survives: a combination of music, dance (in various stages of undress), song, acrobatics and magic, accompanied by ornate sets and fancy lighting. You can combine a visit to a nightclub with a fancy meal or just a drink, or you can simply enjoy the show itself. The price, therefore, depends upon which of these you decide to do, as well as the choice of nighclub. It can vary from 150-550f per person.

The list below covers the great clubs, the "institutions . One sits theater-style in these clubs. Many tourists feel duty-bound to visit one.

Folies Bergère: 32, rue Richer, tel. 42.46.77.11. Cadet metro station.
Casino de Paris: 16, rue de Clichy, tel. 42.82.05.57. Trinité metro station.

Le Milliardaire: 68, rue Pierre Charron, tel. 42.25.25.17. Franklin D. Roosevelt metro station.
Madame Arthur: 75, rue des Martyrs, tel. 42.64.48.27. Pigalle metro station.
Crazy Horse: 12, av. Georges V, 8e, tel. 47.23.32.32. Georges V metro station.
Lido: 116, av. des Champs-Elysées, 8e, tel. 45.63.11.61. Georges V metro station.
Moulin Rouge: Place Blanche, 9e, tel. 46.06.00.19. Blanche metro station.
Paradis Latin: 28, rue du Cardinal-Lemoine, 5e, tel. 43.95.07.07. Cardinal-Lemoine metro station.
Alcazar: 62, rue Mazarine, 6e, tel. 43.29.02.20. Odéon metro station.

Bars

Parisians are wont to spend their evening in a bar. Though the selection ranges from the quiet to the tumultuous, the major ingredients are rather universal: drinks, music and atmosphere. The mysterious spark which makes a bar a phenomenon is the crowd it attracts. The following bars are currently fashionable in Paris:

Hélium: 3, rue des Haudriettes, 3e, tel. 42.72.81.10. A sloppy-looking place, enveloped in a halo since the early 1980s. Good cocktails. Singles.
Harry's Bar: 5, rue Daunou, 2e, tel. 42.61.71.14. A permanent rendez-vous and refuge for "ex-patriot" Americans in Paris. In fact, the story goes that Gershwin composed *An American in Paris* here. Poorly lit (for its own good at times); a jazz pianist performs.
Le Rosebud: 11, rue Delambre, 14^{e}, tel. 43.35.38.54. An urbane, argumentative crowd but superb cocktails.
Bar du Georges V: 331, av. Georges V, 8^{e}, tel. 47.23.54.00. Classy, as opulent as the hotel built around it. Fit for nobility.
Alexandre: 53, av. Georges V, tel. 47.20.17.82. Elegant to the core, something like the inner hall of a throbbing luxury liner.
La Guinness Tavern: 31, rue des Lombards, 1er, tel. 42.33.26.45. The place to drink beer — Guinness, of course.
Balajo: 9, rue de Lappe, 11^{e}, tel. 47.00.07.87. Crowded, hot... the place where the young-at-heart go looking for a mate, and have to dance to do so.
Slow Club: 130, rue de Rivoli, 1^{e}, tel. 42.33.84.30. Go down two levels below the ground floor to a vibrant jazzy atmosphere

and beautiful people dancing bebop.
Caveau de la Huchette: 5, rue de la Huchette, 5e, tel. 43.26.65.05. Sip cocktails in a basement which has existed since the Middle Ages. The venue is well suited to the classical jazz played here. Very special.
Maxim's Bar: 42, av. Gabriel, 8e, tel. 45.61.96.33. More well-known names and pretty faces of high society stars per square meter than anywhere else in town. What with this and the 25 varieties of champagne available at the bar, who pays attention to the pianist!
Sinaloa: 41, rue du Colisée, 8e, tel. 42.89.12.56. Here too, you can see famous faces from the movie and entertainment world — and those who come to see them. Still, the 1930 decor is magnificent and the cocktails excellent. Champagne bar.
H20: 50, rue Godefroy Cavaignac, 11e, tel. 40.09.90.92. Pleasant young crowd — lovers of jazz, rock and cocktails with a South American flavor.
Le Montgolfier: 8, rue Louis-Armand, 11e, tel. 40.60.30.30. Movie style bar. Drink from films while watching short movies and listening to movie soundtracks. For film lovers!
Kitty O'Sheas's: 10, rue des Capucines, 2e, tel. 45.15.08.08. An Irish fortress with all the original trappings, including the beer which comes from Ireland, and Irish tunes in the background.

Discotheques

An international form of entertainment, pursued by those in search of dance, drink and new acquaintances... Many Paris discotheques occasionally host bands and individual artists in special performance. Entrance varies from 50-150f, including the first drink.

La Scala: 188, rue de Rivoli, 1er, tel. 42.61.64.00. Palais-Royal metro station. Mighty sound systems, a gaint video screen, laser light show. Girls enter free on weekdays.
Salle Wagram: 39, av. de Wagram, 17e, tel. 43.80.30.03. Ternes metro station. Modern decor, special light effects, music videos on large screen.
Navy Club: 58, bd. de l'Hôpital, 13e, tel. 45.35.91.94. Three dance floors. Tuesday is "Nostalgia Night", featuring 1960s-style sounds — rock, boogie, bebop, disco.
Les Bains: 7, rue du Bourg l'Abbé, 3e, tel. 48.87.01.80. Etienne Marcel metro station. Used to be the hot spot of the disco scene during the eighties, but is on the way down.

Le Kiss: 26, rue des Lombards, 4e, tel. 48.87.89.64. A wonderful place with a great atmosphere and lots of African and Afro-Jazz bands and music. Has an all-night restaurant.
Les Bus Palladium: 6, rue Fontaine, 9e, tel. 48.74.69.25. Blanche metro station. An established disco which is still going strong, thanks to the famous names in the entertainment and sports world who frequent the place.
Le Fibus: 18, rue du Fg du Temple, 10e, tel. 47.00.78.86. République metro station. A matter of taste, attracts many people from around the city wearing leather suits and shiny studs. Also a "regular" crowd. Heavy rock.
Le Palace: 8, rue du Faubourg-Montmartre, 9e, tel. 42.46.10.87. Rue Montmartre metro station. One of the biggest and most famous discos in the city. Here you can find all types — for better or worse.
La Locomotive: 90, bd. de Clichy, tel. 42.57.37.37. Rue Montmartre metro station. One of the most amazing in the city 28,000 sq/ft (2500 sq/m) of bubbling activity, music, video clips and dancing. Has to be seen to be believed.

Concerts, Opera and Ballet

Paris of recent years is enjoying an extraordinary revival of classical music. Tickets are scarce and reservations are essential even for events not considered major. Lovers of church music will also find their visit to Paris quite fruitful.

Major concert halls

Pleyel: 252, rue du Fg. St.-Honoré, 8e, tel. 45.63.88.73. Ternes metro station. The home of the Paris Symphony Orchestra. Concert information: tel. 45.63.07.96, Sat. and Sun. 11am-5pm.
Théâtre des Champs-Elysées: 15, av. Montaigne, 8e, tel. 47.23.47.77. Alma-Marceau metro station. Hosts visiting performers, a famous orchestra, ballet and more.
Radio-France: 116, av. du Président Kennedy, 16e, tel. 45.24.15.16. Bir-Hakeim metro station. Its concerts are often recorded for radio or live broadcast. Tickets are particularly reasonable, occasionally free.
Gaveau: 45, rue de la Boétie, 8e, tel. 45.63.20.30. Miromesnil metro station. Frequent piano recitals, plush and elegant atmosphere.
Théâtre Musical de Paris: Place du Châtelet, 1er, tel. 42.61.19.83. Châtelet metro station. Once a theater for operettas, now a concert hall for classical music. Information:

tel. 42.61.81.23, 11am-6pm.
L'Opéra: Place de l'Opéra, 8e, tel. 47.42.57.50. Venue for great classical operas and ballets. Opera metro station.
L'Opéra Comique: 5, rue Favart, 9e, tel. 42.96.06.11. Richelieu Drouot metro station. Light opera and operettas, occasional musicals.

Church music

Notre-Dame de Paris: Place de Paris, 4e, tel. 43.26.07.39. Cité metro station. Church organ concert usually every Sun. at 5:45pm. Admission free.
American Church: 65, Quai d'Orsay, 7e, tel. 47.05.07.99. Invalides metro station. Guitar and piano concerts. Information at the church or by phone. Admission free.
L'Eglise des Billettes: 24, rue des Archives, 4e. Hôtel de Ville metro station. Information at the church.
L'Eglise Saint-Etienne du Mont: Place du Panthéon, 6e. Luxembourg metro station. Information at the church.

Theater

Visitors who have no command of French are at a great disadvantage, although, devoted theater lovers will not be dissuaded or deterred. Paris abounds with spirited classical, modern and avant-garde theater in a variety of establishments. The major ones follow:

Comédie-Française: Place du Théâtre-Français, 1er, tel. 45.15.00.15. Palais-Royal metro station. The veteran national theater stages classical and modern productions.
Chaillot: Place Trocadéro, 16e, tel. 47.27.81.15. Trocadéro metro station. A national theater extensively involved in local works. The appointment of the great director Jérôme Sabari, as director has infused new energy into the company. Three halls.
Odéon: Place Paul Claudel, 6e, tel. 43.25.70.32. Odéon metro station. A theater which devotes much of its resources to modern, up-to-date drama.
Cartoucherie: Route du Champ-de-Manœuvres, 12e, tel. 43.74.24.08. Château-de-Vincennes metro station, and bus 112 from there. A famous theater which stages giant avant-garde productions.
Café d'Edgar: 58, bd. Edgar-Quinet, 14e, tel. 43.22.11.02. Edgar-Quinet metro station. Three halls, as many as eight

performances per evening. One of the most famous examples of the cafe-theater.

Café de la Gare: 41, rue du Temple, 3e, tel. 42.78.52.51. Hôtel de Ville metro station. The legendary cafe-theater where many of Paris' most renowned performers began their careers.

Important Phone Numbers

One can obtain a wealth of information of almost anything including emergency services by phone. The various telephone information services are rather efficient in saving runaround, time, and money. For most of the services listed below, the voice at the other end is a recorded message in French or English (sometimes other languages). In order to call outside of Paris, dial 16-1 and then the number.

International calls can be made from public phones by dialing 19 first. Collect calls (known in French as *P.C.V.*) are made from the PTT Communications and Post Agency. Below are few country codes:

U.S.A. 1
Switzerland 41
Spain 34
Germany 49
U.K. 44
Italy 39
Belgium 32
Japan 81

Police — 17.
Fire department — 18.
Ambulance — 43.78.26.26.
Tourist information (in English) — 47.20.60.20.
- (in French) — 47.23.61.72.
Theater and restaurant reservations — 43.59.12.12.
Trains — 42.82.50.50.
Metro and buses — 43.46.14.14.
Charles de Gaulle Airport — 48.62.22.80.
Orly Airport — 48.84.32.10.
Air France — 42.99.24.24.
T.W.A. — 47.20.62.11.
Leisure entertainment information — 47.20.94.94. (French).
— 47.20.88.98. (English).
— 47.20.57.58. (German).
Museum information — 42.78.73.81.
Time — 46.99.84.00.
Wakeup service — 46.88.71.11. (not for use in hotels).
Road conditions — 48.58.33.33.

Motor breakdown service — 47.07.99.99.; 43.31.14.14.
Weather in Paris and vicinity — 45.55.95.90.
Lost-and-found — 45.31.14.80.
Stock market information — 42.60.84.00 (noon-4pm).
Customs information — 42.80.13.26.
International direct dialing — 19.
Telephone information — 12.
Emergency pharmacy — 45.62.02.41.
Hospital (English speaking) — 47.47.53.00.
Emergency nurses — 48.87.77.77.
Baby-sitter reservations — 40.38.46.10; 46.47.89.89.
Poison treatment — 42.05.63.29.
Burn treatment — 47.72.91.91.
Vehicle towing — 42.36.10.00.
Medical service (house calls) — 47.07.77.77.
Emergency dentist — 43.57.51.00 (after 8pm and weekends).
Veterinarian service (house calls) — 42.65.00.91.
Veterinary ambulance — 47.84.55.55.
TV program information — 47.20.02.00.
Horoscope service — 36.69.54.54.

INDEX

INDEX

QUESTIONNAIRE

In our efforts to keep up with the pace and pulse of Paris, we kindly ask your cooperation in sharing with us any information which you may have, as well as your comments. We would greatly appreciate your completing and returning the following questionnaire. Feel free to add additional pages. A complimentary copy of the next edition will be sent to you should any of your suggestions be included.

Our many thanks!

To: Inbal Travel Information (1983) Ltd.
2 Chen Blvd.
Tel Aviv 64071
Israel

Name: ____________________

Address: ____________________

____

Occupation: ____________________

Date of visit: ____________________

____

Purpose of trip (vacation, business, etc.): ____________________

____

____

Comments/Information: ____________________

____

____

____

____

____

____

____

____

____

____

____

____

____

2/90

INBAL Travel Information Ltd.
P.O.B. 39090 Tel Aviv
ISRAEL 61390

NOTES

NOTES